DIXIE DE

of

TRANMERE ROVERS
1923-1925

by

Gilbert Upton

Published by The Author

8 Cumberland Road Southport Merseyside PR8 6NY

1992

DEDICATION

To Jo, Hillary, Stephen and Mum.

And to Dad and Pop (R.I.P.).

Gilbert Upton
Southport
10 June, 1992

First published in Great Britain in 1992 by The Author

ISBN 0 9518648 1 5

DIXIE DEAN OF TRANMERE ROVERS

1923 -1925

CONTENTS

ACKNOWLEDGEMENTS

In writing this book, I have enjoyed the help and support of Peter Bishop, the programme editor at Tranmere Rovers, who gave me the opportunity to publish my articles about Dixie Dean's short but spectacular career at his first Football League club, during the 1989-90 season. And Bernard Jones, too, who provided the 1924-25 teams. We have worked well together now for over seven years and long may it continue.

My thanks, once more, to the printer Mal Halligan, and his team, for his crucial part in the publication of this, my second, book. It has been through Mal's dedication to quality, aided in no small measure by Chris Driver's expertise in converting my BBC "B" computer files to the more modern PC compatible format, that my books have been produced to the highest standard. And, on this occasion, Gerry Solich's superb cover design has made its own vital contribution. To all three, I am eternally grateful.

For their generosity in making their collections available to me, I gratefully acknowledge the contributions of George Higham, for the contemporary programmes, and Ron Kennedy, for the photographs and cuttings from his grandfather, and a team-mate of Dixie, George Jackson. For making Ellis Rimmer's signing on contract available, my thanks to his nephew, Warwick Rimmer. And thanks, too, to Dave Russell for his recollections about his efforts on Dixie's behalf.

I must once again express my gratitude to Wirral Library Services, at the Central Library in Birkenhead, for the use of their local studies material and to their counterparts around the North of England who have so kindly assisted me with my researches.

Finally, my appreciation is extended to those, including Billy Wray, who were so kind about my first book, the history of Tranmere Rovers between 1881 and 1921, and their encouragement for me to come up with another. I had no plans to launch again into print until then. Perhaps this topic is not quite what they expected, but no less welcome for all that, I trust.

INTRODUCTION

When researching the early history of Tranmere Rovers, I inevitably came upon the discovery and rise of Dixie Dean. I grew up with the legend of Dixie Dean in Birkenhead, his home town too, and my own grandfather often spoke about those electric days when the size of the crowd was greatly affected by whether Dixie was playing or not and Prenton Park would ring to the cry of "Give it to Dixie!" I thought little more of it all until I bought Bill Houldin's book, "Up Our Lobby" (first edition), in 1987. It is not a book about football but about life in the early decades of the twentieth century in the tenements of north Birkenhead, known as the Dock Cottages.

As related here in Chapter One, Bill Houldin referred to one of his contemporaries as "Digsy" Dean which quite startled me as this was the William Ralph Dean the world had come to know as "Dixie" Dean. Having corresponded with Bill Houldin to shed further light on these two names, I first made this story public when a letter I wrote to Everton Football Club was published in their match programme of 7 May, 1988, for the visit of Arsenal. This was 60 years (and two days) after Dixie scored his 60th Football League goal against those same opponents, Arsenal.

I subsequently set myself a mini-project to trace Dixie's career at Prenton Park, starting when he joined Tranmere Rovers from Pensby Institute, in November, 1923, until his transfer to Everton, for a Third Division record fee, in March, 1925. The aim was to do this simply for purely personal satisfaction and interest in the details of this first important phase of Dixie's extraordinary career, which had not been fully recorded in the material available. I was certainly not prepared for the subsequent twists and turns in the story. Indeed, when the first article appeared, all my research was not complete. I was expecting to take five or six weeks to finish writing a short set of articles, containing relatively routine detail. It was only as the story unfolded over the next six months that the real surprises emerged, as can be detected in that final paragraph of the first and the passing reference to Dixie's five week injury lay-off in February, 1924, in the second.

My sources were primarily local newspaper archives supplemented by the interviews Bob Azurdia, of BBC Radio Merseyside, had with Dixie, first broadcast in January, 1978, when he was 71 years old. There was also his biography by Nick Walsh, published in 1977. When I compared them with what I found in the newspapers, there were clear and obvious discrepancies which decided me to pursue the wages and transfer issues in the archives of The Football League. Again, the evidence did not marry up with the "official" version, as it were.

Because, over the years, Dixie had always made it perfectly clear he had been "diddled" by Tranmere Rovers, and their secretary-manager, Bert Cooke, in particular, first over wages and then over his signing on fee when he joined Everton (and his insistence that he had been hospitalised by Davy Parkes of Rochdale), I wrote up my findings. First published in a series of articles which appeared in the match programmes of Tranmere Rovers between November, 1989, and May, 1990, they did not seek to diminish Dixie Dean—the legend, the legacy or the man. He had not set out to create those differences with his first League club which, quite clearly, were very real to him. In any case, his achievements are incomparable and there is no-one now who believes that they can ever be approached, never mind exceeded.

It is sad that, from when he was a very young man to the day he died, nothing happened to change his mind. There was never the opportunity to explain to him how things might have differed from his own recollections. Despite this, he was big enough to accept the helping hand extended to him in later life by Rovers' manager (1961-69) and, subsequently, general manager, Dave Russell.

Whilst I took great care about how I wrote up my findings in the articles, I also believe that no person, no event, no so-called fact is immune from new research and revaluation. If an alternative version of long past events is brought into the light of day by new evidence, it has to be treated on its merits. As well as bringing together, for the first time, Dixie's full record at Tranmere Rovers, those articles also contained an alternative version of some of the important events between November, 1923, and March, 1925 and the correction of some of the previously published detail.

The other side of the coin is that, by revisiting those contemporary reports about the young Dixie Dean, starting his career with a lowly Third Division team that was, frankly, a poor one, his legend will be further embellished. The sheer excitement and exhilaration, the power and the rampant athleticism of this young man, who was barely eighteen years old when he joined Everton, is still there to be enjoyed and wondered at. Once a first team regular for Rovers, in September, 1924, his fame preceded him so that, wherever he played in a Rovers shirt, they knew that here was a coming star.

Some of this can be re-captured by looking at the local newspapers covering Rovers' opponents. Perhaps none did it better than the Halifax Daily Courier & Guardian which anticipated his coming and then experienced the kind of devastation that Dixie would wreak on defences over the next fifteen years.

This book, therefore, is that collection of programme articles (with corrections), together with other material which could not be found space within the natural confines with which the programme editor, Peter Bishop, has to work. There are, too, three later articles about "Dixie's Return", "Rovers' Youngest" and one of Dixie's early professional mentors, Stan Sayer. It does not attempt to repeat the wealth of biographical detail about his early life, his career at Everton, Notts County and Sligo and then his declining years, which are well covered elsewhere.

I hope that, taken as a whole, I have been able to do something which may have seemed unlikely and add lustre to the Dixie Dean legend. Just as importantly, I trust I have restored the reputation of Tranmere Rovers Football Club over their handling of their greatest ever player, past, present or, very probably, future.

Gilbert Upton
Southport
10 June, 1992

CHAPTER 1

WILLIAM RALPH DEAN

The exploits of Tranmere Rovers' greatest ever player are fully documented when it comes to the glittering career he had at Everton, winning every major honour the game then had to offer. Quite rightly so, as they were of epic proportions. There could be no better comment on them than Dixie's own during his 1978 interviews on Radio Merseyside. He was asked by Bob Azurdia if he thought his 60 Football League goals in one season would ever be beaten. *"Yes"*, was his deadpan reply, *"I think it will. There's only one man can do it. That's that feller that walks on the water. I think he's about the only one."*

Although throughout his career he was known as "Dixie" Dean, it was a nickname he had some distaste for, preferring to be Bill Dean. The usual story about how he became to be known as "Dixie", repeated by Nick Walsh on page 40 of his biography, tells that his swarthy appearance and black curly hair put fans in mind of the American coloured folks from down South in Dixie. It has always seemed a little far-fetched yet makes for a good yarn and could explain, given contemporary attitudes, Dean's feelings towards it. It was only recently I found the true story behind the name "Dixie".

In 1987, I bought a book, published in 1985 by Wirral Libraries called *"Up our Lobby"* by another Birkonian, Bill Houldin, a contemporary and neighbour of the young Dean in the north end of town. In there, on page 39, he refers to Dean as DIGSY and the startling fact hit me that this was where DIXIE must have come from. Bill Houldin recalled:

> *Without a shadow of doubt, the most famous name to play for Wirral Railway F.C. was an ex-railway man himself and the son of an engine driver whose engine literally passed the ground many times daily.*
>
> *Nobody could have ever envisaged that Billy, or "Digsy" Dean, as he was called, would in a few short years be world famous as "Dixie" Dean of Everton and England.*

It immediately struck me that "Dixie" was an obvious corruption of "Digsy" arising from the similarity when spoken or, more likely, shouted.

The Birkenhead News of Wednesday, 28 November, 1923, reported Rovers' historic signing of the young Dean and, probably for the first time ever, the soon to be immortal name of Dixie Dean appeared in print. It also makes it clear that the name "Dixie" was already his when he was still only sixteen years old (the report wrongly gives Dixie's age as seventeen) and was not first given to him by the fans at Prenton Park. By implication, the report tells us he had had that name, probably in its original "Digsy" form, since he played as a schoolboy. It ran:

3

During the last few days, Tranmere Rovers, following their recent signing of Edwards the Bebington youth, have added to their list two seventeen-year-old players who have been distinguishing themselves in local junior circles. One of the signings is C. Millington, a cousin of Joe Mercer, the old Rovers centre-half, who has been assisting Ellesmere Port in the West Cheshire League. He fills the central position in the half-line, and although only seventeen years of age he is 6ft. 1in. in height and weighs 11st. 4lbs. Dixie Dean, the other signing, a former Birkenhead Schoolboy, capped this season's performances on Saturday last by scoring four goals for Pensby Institute.

I wrote to Bill Houldin, who still lives in Birkenhead, to ask him about "Digsy" and "Dixie" and my theory about the former getting corrupted into the latter and being taken up by the journalists. He sent me the following letter:

The name "Digsy" was just one that we grew up with and so never questioned. However, your query prompted me to do a little bit of research and referred to the Birkenhead News report of Bill Dean's funeral. The lady quotes a lady contemporary of Bill's. When questioned about the name "Digsy" she said "When Bill Dean was doing the chasing in a game of "tag" he would catch a young lady and he would dig his fist into the girl's back and for his pains acquired the name "Digsy". (Note: The Birkenhead News' report spells it "Diggzie"!).

The few old neighbours of our's and Dean's I have spoken to have dismissed out of hand any suggestion that "Dixie" had any connotations of colour. I too say this is bunk. Your theory of the combination of sound and journalistic licence is correct.

It is notable that, throughout, Mr Houldin refers to Bill Dean which, to me, gives his evidence that extra touch of authenticity—if it were needed at all. It also fits the report from November, 1923, regarding him having had such a nickname since his days as a schoolboy.

One other fascinating insight into Dixie's career at Prenton Park can be adduced from the evocative Birkenhead News' cartoon of Rovers' squad published on 11 October, 1924 (see page 34). Whilst other players were shown with the ball at their feet, the seventeen-year-old Dixie Dean, by now established in the first XI, curly hair and all, was shown demonstrating his prowess at heading the ball. With 27 goals in 30 Football League games before his record £3,000 transfer to Everton on 16 March, 1925, no wonder the cry *"Give it to Dixie"* rang round Prenton Park.

A biography of Dixie, by Nick Walsh, was published in 1977 but his time with the Rovers was not covered in any depth and contained many inaccuracies. They include the erroneous version of the origin of "Dixie" and the claim that he signed for Rovers when he had just turned sixteen, in January, 1923, having previously played for them as an amateur. As the story of Dixie's career at Prenton Park has not been fully documented before, it is hoped to rectify matters through a short series of articles which will appear in Rovers' matchday programmes over the coming weeks.   (First published 7 November, 1989)

4

CHAPTER 2

FIRST IMPRESSIONS

I t was Rovers' talent scout and former player from the 1890s and early 1900s, Jack "Dump" Lee, who is credited with persuading Dixie to sign for Tranmere Rovers but it can hardly be said that he discovered him. Dixie had been scoring goals all his young life and had represented Birkenhead Schoolboys when aged thirteen in 1920.

He scored all four goals in the 4-0 win over Bootle Boys on 27 November, 1920, one in the 1-1 draw with Bebington on 20 December and two in the 4-2 win over Southport on 27 December when Ellis Rimmer, who was to follow him in wearing a Tranmere Rovers and an England shirt, scored the other two. On 24 November, 1923, the Saturday prior to his signing for Rovers, Dixie notched four goals for Pensby Institute in a 6-1 win over Upton in the Wirral Combination. As the main contributor to their 42 goals in 11 games, Dixie arrived at Prenton Park with something of a reputation in the town.

On 1 December, 1923, within days of joining the club, on amateur forms, Dixie was making his début for the Second XI in the Cheshire County League against Whitchurch. The team for Dixie's first appearance in a Tranmere Rovers shirt was:

> Wilde; Lewis Naylor; Ashmore Millington Hawarden;
> Edwards Rothwell Dean Littlehales Evans.

Aged just 16 years 313 days, he scored Rovers' only goal in a 1-3 defeat by a team which included his schoolboy partner, Ellis Rimmer. He certainly made an immediate impression and the Birkenhead News' match reporter, known only as "C.D.A.", glowingly recorded Dixie's début and his first senior goal:

> *Dean was every inch a complete success. Though only young, he is tall and unusually well built, and carries his 12 stone with ease and grace. He showed himself to be a bustler and an opportunist— but not that alone, for he fed his wings and plied his partners in a style which suggests that with the right encouragement he will flourish into a player who would be an asset to any side . . . Dean received from Rothwell, and went right through, and from a sharp angle, put the ball into the net. Towards the end, Dean went down on his own, and going at a great pace, sent in from a difficult angle. The ball hit the upright with a force that seemed to suggest that it was trying to uproot the woodwork.*

Even in his first game, young Dixie's abilities were noted by the opposition reporter as these comments from the Whitchurch Herald, in which his goal was described as *"a daisy cutter"*, highlight:

The new man Dean, a product of local junior circles, was putting up a remarkably good show.

A week later, the News' sports editor underlined the potential of Rovers' latest acquisition:

I am given to understand Dean was the "star" attraction. Splendidly endowed physically he has height and weight and if somewhat lacking in polish—this can easily be benefited by careful coaching—he has got one strong point, and that is his direct shooting. And the power he imparts to his drives can best be gauged in reference to one drive last week that hit the woodwork and prompted the explanation by colleague, "C.D.A.", that the upright was nearly uprooted.

Later in the month, against Wallasey United on 27 December, 1923, "C.D.A." noted *"Dean was again the most conspicuous player of the afternoon's play"*. In his first nine games for the Reserves, Dixie scored eight goals, became the penalty taker, continued to impress and was called to make his first team début on Wednesday, 9 January, 1924, at inside-right. It was in the Liverpool Senior Cup and Dixie was, once more, on the scoresheet with the first goal in the 4-2 away win over New Brighton. The team and other scorers were:

Mitchell; G Jackson Stuart(1); Buchan Halstead Campbell;
Moreton Dean(1) Sayer Hilton(1) Cartman(1).

Dixie's goal was described in the Birkenhead News like this:

Five minutes had elapsed when Dean lifted the ball neatly over Jones' head, swerved to the left and lobbed in a high dropping shot which deceived Mehaffy by curling under the bar, and the Rovers were "one up".

The following Saturday, 12 January, 1924, Dixie made his Football League début, also at inside-right, but there was to be no fairy-tale start. The youngest player ever to appear for Tranmere Rovers in the Football League, he was 16 years 355 days, he played well in a rather poor First XI beaten 1-5 by Rotherham County in the Third Division (Northern Section):

Mitchell; G Jackson Stuart(1); Campbell Halstead Buchan;
Moreton Dean Sayer Beswick Cartman.

The next week he was back in the Second XI and soon back amongst the goals. In February, his progress was noted in the Birkenhead Advertiser in these terms:

In the centre, Dean is still going strong and he is one of the most promising players on the books.

He was by now attracting the attention of writers from outside Birkenhead too, a good example being when he played against Altrincham on 9 February, 1924. The reporter from the Altrincham, Hale & Bowdon Guardian wrote:

Although the ground was heavy, the game was remarkably fast... The young centre-forward (Dean) of the Rovers was responsible for a fine bit of individual work by breaking through the defence and scoring a splendid goal for his side—it was certainly a very brilliant effort by the Rovers' youthful centre-forward.

Following this game, Dixie had a five week lay-off and scored in only five of the remaining sixteen games he played in. Mind you, that included five in the game against Middlewich with Ellis Rimmer, who had joined Rovers for a trial period, scoring the other two. Writing later in the Birkenhead News' end of season review, "R.E.T." made out that Dixie had *"created a record goal-scoring feat for the club"* with his five goals but Harry Fishwick had once scored six for the First XI in The Combination, in October, 1908, against Whitchurch.

Towards the end of the season, he made two more Football League appearances in the First XI. With Rovers having to play four games in five days and injuries to Buchan, Campbell and Moreton, he was pressed into service as an emergency left half for the re-arranged game at Rochdale on Tuesday, 22 April, 1924. Rovers lost 0-1 and Dixie made his first acquaintance with Rochdale's centre-half, Davy Parkes, of whom more later. The team was:

Mitchell; G Jackson Stuart; Checkland Halstead Dean;
Hayes Brown Sayer Littlehales Cartman.

Two weeks later, on 3 May, 1924, in the last game of the season, Rovers faced Wolverhampton Wanderers who were about to return to the Second Division after one brief season in the Third Division (North). With injuries to Halstead and Brown, Dixie, who was down to play at Altrincham, was, at the last minute, given the role of centre-forward in a senior game for the first time:

Mitchell; G Jackson Stuart; Buchan Leary Campbell;
Moreton Sayer Dean Littlehales Cartman.

Before a crowd of 11,965 (gate £627), Rovers earned an unexpected draw, 0-0. Dixie was unusually nervous, miskicking several times when he might have done better with more experience and composure. He was reported to have found the seasoned opposing pivot, Caddick, *"too much for him"*. No doubt it was an early lesson well learned and a valuable increment in his store of match experience.

(First published 2 December, 1989)

7

Birkenhead Schoolboys XI which defeated Bootle Schoolboys 4-0, 4 December, 1920.
BACK: Mr Bethel, Mr Lewis, H.Zinges, E.Thomas, L.Harris, Mr McTear, Mr Taylor;
MIDDLE: F.Jones, J.Goodchild, W.Smith;
FRONT: W.Hocker, N.Cavanagh, W.Dean(4), R.Philip, E.Rimmer.
(Birkenhead News)

CHAPTER 3

CREATING A BIG IMPRESSION

S till only seventeen years old at the start of the 1924-25 season, and now a full time professional, Dixie began in the Reserve XI, despite scoring six times in three pre-season public trial games between the Blues and the Reds. The club was aware that they had a huge talent on their hands but declined to push him into the hurly burly of Third Division football too soon, even in the face of clamour from Roverites for Dixie's promotion.

When the Cheshire County League fixtures got under way, after failing to score in the opener against Port Vale Reserves, Dixie set the world alight in his next two games. In the game at Nantwich, on Wednesday, 3 September, 1924, Dixie scored all four goals in the 4-2 win which drew this prescient and illuminating comment from the Birkenhead News' reporter, "..Dixie Dean, the giant limbed boy centre forward, who many critical judges consider has a remarkable future before him..".

After missing the game at Stalybridge Celtic on the following Saturday, because of an injury he received at Nantwich, Dixie went one better when he scored five in the 7-2 mid-week thrashing of Whitchurch at Prenton Park. He had now reached the point where his claim to be in the First XI could no longer be ignored. Letters started appearing in the local papers, like this one in the Birkenhead News of 10 September, 1924:

> I offer the following line as possessing both youth, speed and weight coupled with experience, the main essentials of a forward line: Birtles, Sayer, Dean, Brown, Griffiths. Act quickly, Rovers, and the public will support you. Yours, etc., "H.G."

The News added its own weight to the campaign with these comments on 13 September, 1924:

> The local boy, Dean, is not only the talk of the town but in various parts of the country by reason of his play and scoring feats.

Dixie's moment of destiny came that Saturday, 13 September, 1924. He travelled with the first team to Doncaster and, when current Irish international Jack Brown cried off injured, Dixie was finally given the centre forward spot which would be his until his move to Everton six months later. It was also the game in which Ellis Rimmer, who had signed for Rovers the day before, made his League debut. His chance soon came to him when Billy Crewe, who lived in Wolverhampton, telegraphed from Sheffield station to say he was stranded.

After the disappointment of the 0-2 defeat at Doncaster, Dixie played his final Cheshire County League game on the Monday at Witton Albion. On 20 September, 1924, came his own first League goal, in the 1-0 victory over Southport:

Rovers' goal, when it came about five minutes from the close of play, was a good one. It happened this way. A misunderstanding occurred between Mulligan and Allen, enabling Moreton to slip through and centre to Dean. Dean took the ball in his stride, cleverly eluded Allen, who had come back to retrieve the situation, and slipped the ball into the net. Rovers' supporters were frantic with excitement, and the cheering was sustained practically to the end of the game.

(Birkenhead News).

The Cheshire side took pride in the fact that they had lowered the colours of the League leaders and there was a feeling of jubilation in the camp because Dean, their young centre forward, had done the needful in the scoring line.

(Southport Visiter).

In his first ten League games, nine goals were scored. Dixie Dean had well and truly arrived. When, on 22 October, England played an international match against Ireland at Goodison Park, Bert Cooke, Rovers' secretary-manager, was there and was the centre of attraction for the representatives of the big First Division clubs. They had already heard about the genius of Dean, now being referred to as the *"talented boy leader"* and noted for his *"aggressiveness and shooting powers in front of goal"*.

Cooke was not having anything to do with their overtures and, so it would seem, was delighting at being in a position where, for once, he could twist tigers' tails. After the international, one unnamed party (thought to have been from Preston North End, with whom Rovers had enjoyed fixtures going back to their earliest days in the 1880s) decided he would seize the opportunity to proposition Bert Cooke by saying he had his chequebook with him and was ready to do business. With more than a twinkle in his eye, Bert reputedly told him, *"Seeing that it is your club, the Rovers might consider, if the offer is big enough, letting you have a photo of Dean."* (The full version of this report is in Appendix D). Dixie's own riposte was to score his first League hat-trick, on the following Saturday, at home to Hartlepools United, and so foster even keener interest in him.

Dixie was now in full flow but an ankle injury, when tackled by full-back Stirling in the fourth minute of the game at Rochdale on 1 November, 1924, was to slow him down. He struggled through to the interval and actually managed to head Rovers' goal but missed the second half. The following week, against Darlington, he should never have played and so aggravated the injury that it put him out of the F A Cup tie with Crewe Alexandra on 15 November. Whilst he recovered in time for the replay, he was to go five games without scoring, including the two F A Cup games against Southport, until he found the net twice against Chesterfield on 6 December.

Nick Walsh's biography shows that Dixie scored one goal for Rovers in the F A Cup, but this conclusively is not so. He did, however, score against First Round opponents Crewe but that was in the Cheshire Senior Medals tie on 25 September, 1924, which is where the error must have come from.

By the time of the game against Chesterfield on 6 December, 1924, Dixie's style was clear:

> *Play had been in progress ten minutes, when Brown tricked Thompson and pushed the ball up the middle for Dean to round first Dennis and then Saxby. Dean, in his individual burst, had worked to the inside-right position but although badly angled he made a fierce cross shot that travelled into the net at a great pace. Five minutes from time, Moreton and Brown got away on the home right, and from the wingman's centre, Dean brought the ball under control, rounded Abbott (CH) and then Saxby (RB) and put on a clever concluding point.*

(Birkenhead News).

Across in Chesterfield, there was clear evidence that Dixie's value was mounting by the week:

> *It was said that the directors of Tranmere Rovers F.C. duly celebrated the Rovers' fine win immediately after the match.*

> *It was also said that whichever club wanted Dixie Dean, the Rovers' seventeen years-old but clever centre forward, would have to pay another round thousand pounds for him now. Chesterfield could do with the services of such a player—but not at an expenditure of £3,000.*

(Derbyshire Times).

Only two weeks before that, his value had been put at £2,000 as this report in the Southport Visiter after the F A Cup replay on 3 December, 1924, indicates:

> *The Rovers side included Dean, a young centre forward, for whom, it is stated, the Birkenhead club have been offered £2,000. He was, however, seldom in the picture, for Little had him in almost complete subjection and, in addition, he appeared to be beaten by the pace of the ground.*

It was still very true that, in his first three months, Dixie had created a huge impression and was the rising star of the Third Division. Local papers elsewhere either wrote in expectation of his coming and then the way he had terrorised his opposition defences or, if Dixie did not score, take some delight and praise the performance of the local centre-half. As a prime example of the first approach, read what the Halifax Daily Courier & Guardian had to say before the match on 20 December, 1924:

'WARE DEAN
Tranmere's Centre Forward Prodigy

'..if rumour be true, the Rovers are the most "watched" team in the country, for quite a crowd of League clubs have sent their scouts on the trail of young "Dixie" Dean, the youthful centre forward of the Rovers who this season has sprung into the limelight with similar meteoric brilliance that Wheelhouse did 12 months ago. Dean, who is a native of Birkenhead, is only 18 years of age, and is a product of the Wirral Combination. He scored 23 goals towards the close of last season with Tranmere's second string and this campaign has been drafted into the first team with such success that he now rivals the goalscoring record of Brown of Darlington. Town would do well to keep a sharp eye on this prodigy.

And after the game:

..Town's defence crumbled in front of the swift thrusts of Dean and his men.. ..Dean dribbled half the length of the field to equalise.. ..Dean is without doubt a coming star..

The News' own report gives an even fuller flavour of the Dean treatment of opposing defences:

Dean (who) had been well boosted in both the local paper and the Halifax programme .. got a brilliant equalising goal and brought forth the plaudits of the home crowd to show that the good things foretold of him were not idle gossip. Moreton gave to Dean, who was standing on the half way line, and in a position that threatened no danger. Duckett challenged Dean but was brushed aside, and then Hall and Lees suffered a similar fate when trying to bowl over the boy leader, who used his weight to great advantage. As Fryer ran out, Dean, from about fifteen yards out, in the coolest manner conceivable, drove the leather low into the net to crown a brilliant individual effort. Four minutes later, Moreton raced away on the right and put in a high centre which Dean headed in clever fashion into the top corner of the net.

Plans had to be laid to thwart Dixie, who was effectively the only threat from Rovers, and there was almost an anguished cry of unfair play from the Birkenhead Advertiser when Southport found a way to combat his threat in the F A Cup:

Regarding Dean, the columns of publicity given to his abilities as a goalscorer have resulted in the opposing centre-half being told off to act as a sort of policeman, and on Saturday Little followed him with a persistency which, to Dean, must have been rather annoying and uncanny. Wherever the home centre was, so also was Little, and the former was given very few chances to shine, greatly to the detriment of his side. Little played his shadowing part well.

Tranmere Rovers First XI, 1923-24

BACK: Jackson, Buchan, Halstead, Mitchell, Stuart, Campbell, Lt.Col. W.H.Stott *(Chairman)*
FRONT: Beswick, Brown, Sayer, Cartman, J.Hayes.

(Peter Bishop)

Tranmere Rovers Second XI, 1923-24

No Dixie but including Charlie Millington who signed for Rovers at the same time.

BACK: Checkland, Lewis, Millington, Wilde, Naylor, Hawarden;

FRONT: J.Hayes, Littlehales, Rothwell, F.A.Hayes, Unknown.

(Peter Bishop)

14

Tranmere Rovers First XI, just prior to Dixie breaking into it in September, 1924:
BACK: Crewe, Jackson, Mitchell (captain), Halstead, Stuart, Campbell;
FRONT: Moreton, Brown, Sayer, Littlehales, Cartman.

(Peter Bishop)

The first known photograph of Dixie Dean in a Tranmere Rovers shirt v Hartlepools United on 25 October, 1924, the day of Dixie's first League hat-trick:
BACK: Checkland, Jackson, Mitchell, Halstead, Stuart, Campbell
FRONT: Cartman, Sayer, Lt.Col. Stott (Chairman), Dean, Brown, Rimmer.

(Ron Kennedy)

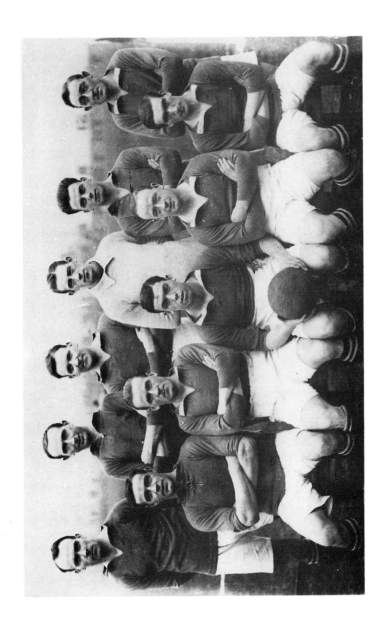

Tranmere Rovers v Halifax Town, 20 December, 1924, at Halifax.
It seems likely Dixie is wearing a red shirt!
BACK: Jeffs, Stuart, Halstead, Briggs, Naylor, Rutter;
FRONT: Moreton, Brown, Dean, Sayer, Cartman.

Bert Cooke, Rovers' secretary-manager, 1912-1935.
Almost without exception, he struck this pose, and wore the same flat cap and watch chain,
in a whole series of team portraits over this period.
(Peter Bishop)

Billy Gaskill, Rovers' team coach in Dixie's time.
He had been a player in the 1890s and team coach since 1912.
(Peter Bishop)

George Jackson poses before town end goal at Prenton Park.
Note the very poor conditions under foot and the original changing pavilion.
(Ron Kennedy)

When Rovers had visited Darlington, on 8 November, 1924, Dixie drew a blank as Rovers went down 0-1. The Northern Echo's response was to laud the part played by the Quakers' centre-half, Robinson, yet their comments do underline how quickly Dixie's reputation was growing well beyond Birkenhead:

> *Darlington's half-backs were a splendid trio, Robinson playing remarkably well. He kept Dean, the Rovers' centre-forward, who, by reason of his recent goal-scoring feats, has attracted much attention, in complete subjection and chopped up attack after attack.*

The fans too knew just how important Dixie was to Rovers and a couple of them reflected their views in this letter to the Advertiser on 24 December, 1924:

> *May we suggest the following forward line for Tranmere Rovers: Moreton, Brown, Dean, Rothwell, and Cartman? Given a trial, we are sure it would be an improvement on the whole team, providing they play to Dean.*
> *Yours, etc., TWO ROVERITES.*

On 10 January, 1925, twelve days before his eighteenth birthday, Dixie was injured after 5 minutes with another kick on the ankle and missed the second half of the game at Walsall. He struggled through the next two games without scoring when it was evident to everyone that he was not yet back at his best. Even so, from the Chesterfield game, Dixie scored eighteen times in his final seventeen games for Rovers. They included two more hat-tricks, against Barrow and Rochdale, and another marvellous goal at Hartlepools, on 28 February, 1925:

> *The second half was 18 minutes old when Littlehales gained possession and slipped the ball into the middle for Dean who was about 40 yards from goal. The visiting leader at once burst through, avoided a back set for him by Storer, rounded first Smith(E) and then Gray and, as Cowell was emerging from his charge, Dean crashed the ball into the net well out of the reach of the keeper. When Dean took up his position for the restart of the game, he was given a great ovation by the crowd and thereafter Dean's every action was applauded.*

(Birkenhead News).

Marvellous as this goal was, it was just one of the many where he took the ball from the halfway line, brushing aside and beating defenders on the way, before powering his shot home. Such was the excitement he caused, the club appealed to spectators not to be unfair to the boy wonder and expect him to score every time he was in a shooting position. By now, such was the excitement he generated the cry of "Give it to Dixie" (originally a political slogan in the U.S.A.) reverberated around Prenton Park and became a part of Birkonian patois, even to this day.

Dixie's last appearance for Rovers at Prenton Park was against Rochdale on 7 March, 1925. He signed off with a hat-trick against his great adversary, Davy Parkes, but there is an element of generosity about the attribution of his first, as this report from the Rochdale Observer (similar to those in the Birkenhead local papers) portrays:

> *Dean bagged a couple of goals for Tranmere, and thus secured a victory for his side.*

> *With the game nine minutes old, Tranmere secured the lead in lucky fashion. Following a throw-in near the half-way line the ball slipped down the right wing for Cartman to leave Stirling behind and close in for goal. Mason went over to give challenge, but missed the ball with his lunge, and Cartman shot in with three inside men closing in on goal. Moody punched out straight ahead, and the ball went to Dean, who shot in along the ground. Had the ball been allowed to take its course, it would have rolled just outside the far post, but STIRLING, apparently under the impression either that it would go inside the post or that an opponent would get to it, kicked wildly, and shot into the top rigging.*

It was after this game that "Forward" wrote about the importance of Dixie to Rovers:

> *The forwards were spasmodic and without Dean as a goalscorer they would be a negligible quantity. "Dixie" is not only the life and soul of the line, but a terror when near goal.*

> (Birkenhead Advertiser, 11 March, 1925).

Within a week, Dixie, now undoubtedly the hottest property in the Football League and the target of the leading First Division clubs, had departed. As the Birkenhead News' reporter "R.E.T." had noted and recorded, *"Dean was as well watched on the field as he was from the stands."* When the transfer deadline became imminent, it was Everton who made the decisive move which took Dixie to Goodison Park to join the only club he ever really wanted to play for. The rest, as they say, is History.

(First published 6 & 20 February, 1990)

CHAPTER 4

INDELIBLE IMPRESSIONS

Dixie's last game was away at Darlington, on 14 March, 1925, where he scored Rovers' orphan goal in a 1-2 defeat. It was otherwise not a very notable goal, as Dixie's goals went, with the opposing 'keeper, Crumley, fumbling the ball into the net when Dixie headed in an Ellis Rimmer cross, midway through the first half. Dixie was later injured and made his final exit in a Tranmere Rovers shirt with twenty minutes to go:

> *Following a run and centre by Rimmer, the Rovers were then enabled to open the scoring through Dean, who, after thirty-five minutes play, headed the ball past Crumley, the latter fumbling the leather, greatly to the disappointment of the crowd.*

(Birkenhead Advertiser, 18 March, 1925).

The local paper in Darlington saw the incident slightly differently:

> *The Darlington goalkeeper (Crumley) made one tragic error and it was this that led to Tranmere taking the lead. DEAN had headed the ball goalwards and it bounced immediately in front of the goalkeeper, who appeared to have it well covered, but to the crowd's surprise the ball passed Crumley on his left side and entered the net.*
>
> *Robinson gave Dean, Tranmere's goal scoring centre forward, little scope.*

(The Northern Echo, 16 March, 1925).

Dixie spent the following Monday afternoon, the players' day off and, more significantly, the transfer deadline, at the cinema. We know, from his radio interviews, that he favoured cowboy and adventure pictures, *"but not love stories and all that caper"*. From what was playing in Birkenhead that week, it seems most likely he was at The Scala, in Argyle Street, watching *"Rupert of Henzau"*.

When he returned home, his mother told him that the Everton secretary, Mr Tom McIntosh, was waiting for him down at the Woodside Hotel. Everton were badly in need of someone to score goals and Dixie was just what they were looking for, and how. It seems well established that centre forwards were, as ever, at a premium if this editorial from the Nelson Leader, at the time of Rovers' visit in February, 1925, is anything to go by:

> *Football Gossip*
>
> *There are still nearly three months to go to the end of the football season, but it is perfectly obvious just now that certain clubs regard the weeks remaining as full of importance. During the past few days there has been quite a lot of transfer news. Clubs in the running for championships, and those in danger of relegation, have been*

specially busy signing new men to help them to attain their desires
or to avoid the fate which threatens. As it is the habit to regard goal-
getters as of much more importance than goal-savers—though I
cannot imagine why—it may be more than a coincidence that the
recent transfer activity has specially concerned centre-forwards.

The move to Everton was just what Dixie had always dreamed would happen and, despite the efforts of Bert Cooke to get Dixie to show an interest in Newcastle United when Rovers were away at Ashington, no other club would have a look in, if Dixie was going to have any say in the matter. He ran all the way back into town and signed for Everton without giving it a further thought. He never even asked about the financial arrangements. He told Bob Azurdia it was *"the greatest delight of my life"*.

The exact fee paid to Rovers was never made public but the Advertiser's football correspondent, "Forward", claimed to have it from *"a very reliable authority"* that it was £2,900, then a record for any Third Division player, the record fee in the Football League then being £5,500. His rival in the Birkenhead News, "R.E.T.", reported the fee was *"as near as makes no matter £3,000"*. This was just about the sum the directors needed to clear the club's overdraft and, at last, relieved them of the personal guarantees they had given to the bank.

Dixie had spent just sixteen months at Prenton Park and, as well as leaving an indelible impression on all Roverites and upon the spectators at the many other grounds where he played, he was now to go on to be the greatest exponent of the art and science of centre forward that the game in this country has ever seen. For Roverites, there was the consolation that he had joined a local club where they would still be able to watch him but there was the corresponding concern that Prenton Park gates would suffer as a result.

Dixie's record for Rovers in 1924-25 is detailed in Appendix B and the First XIs he played in are in Appendix C. He had contributed 27 out of the First XI's 48 League and Cup goals (44 in games he actually played in) and, if it had not been for his remarkable record, Rovers would surely have finished at the foot of the table. As it was, they finished next to bottom and re-election was by no means certain although, thankfully, it did come to pass. His total tally of appearances and goals scored in all games while with Tranmere Rovers is given in Appendix C. Rovers' record at the end of the 1924-25 season in the Third Division (North) was to be:

			Home					Away			
P	W	D	L	F	A	W	D	L	F	A	Pts
Pre-Dixie's transfer	30	8	3	4	31	20	2	1	12	13	29	24
Post-Dixie's transfer	12	3	0	3	9	9	1	0	5	6	20	8
	42	11	3	7	40	29	3	1	17	19	49	32

Before leaving this chapter in Dixie's career, it is worth looking at how he scored his goals. Whilst the Birkenhead News' cartoon of 11 October, 1924, shows Dixie leaping to head the ball and his power in the air was to become legendary, the statistics show that, during his time with Rovers, he scored but one quarter of his goals with headers. The rest were shots and penalties. His renown at Prenton Park was far more for his exciting individual forays on goal from just inside his opponents' half and the power of his shooting, as described when he scored at Hartlepools, on 28 February, 1925. Indeed, shortly after the move to Everton, "Forward" commented upon the *"Toffies'"* rush to play Dixie in the first team and then their failure to play to Dixie's strengths, in these terms:

> *I notice he (Dean) has been chosen to play for the first team at Woolwich today and I think this is a big mistake, as he had an ankle injury at Darlington last Saturday from which he cannot have entirely recovered and, on the other hand, the Everton directors would have been wise to nurse him in their Central League team.*

(Birkenhead Advertiser, 21 March, 1925).

> *Unless he is given the right type of passes to enable him to go through the opposing backs he cannot be expected to show the same form as he did at Prenton Park.*

(Birkenhead Advertiser, 1 April, 1925).

Events have proved that Everton did get the best out of Dixie but it is an intriguing thought that, if he had gone to one of the many other First Division clubs who tried to sign him, he might not have become the legend he now is. However, there was one famous club which was not interested in him. At one time, there was a framed telegram displayed in the boardroom at Goodison Park which read:

> *(TO) COOKE STOP TRANMERE ROVERS STOP*
> *NOT INTERESTED IN DEAN STOP*
> *HERBERT CHAPMAN STOP ARSENAL STOP*

Quite how and why what was obviously the property of Rovers came to be acquired by the Everton directors is a mystery. Perhaps, if they still have it, they might be asked to return it! It is also another clear indication that Rovers' directors, through Bert Cooke, were actively seeking a lucrative transfer deal with one of the wealthy clubs. And Dixie's own position had to be taken into account too. He was undeniably a great prospect and the time had come where it would have been unfair not to let him go to a first class club to develop his career and increase his earnings. As "R.E.T." wrote at the time:

> *Dixie is a born and natural footballer, and if he steers clear of injury I believe he will achieve the highest honours the game has to bestow upon him.*

How right he was and it shows just what a fund of goodwill accompanied Dixie when he crossed the water for Goodison Park. He left with the best wishes of the club and its fans. He must also have had the gratitude of the directors who, in one smart piece of business, had paid off all but the smallest part of the club's overdraft and left the way clear for them to pay off the remaining debt on the purchase of Prenton Park—you might say Dixie paid for Prenton Park!

For all that, for much of the rest of his life, he seemed to have harboured a somewhat embittered attitude towards his first professional club. Tranmere fans will always be immensely proud that their club gave Dixie to the world and it has always hurt to think that, for so long, his abiding sentiment towards the Rovers, so often publicly expressed, was so grudging.

(First published 20 & 23 February, 1990)

The young William Ralph Dean, black wavy hair and all!
Born 22 January, 1907
Died 1 March, 1980

CHAPTER 5

MISTAKEN IMPRESSIONS

In Dixie's eyes, there were two great *"breaches of faith"*, as Nick Walsh described them, which led him to harbour such long and heart felt antipathies towards Tranmere Rovers. Inevitably, they concerned money and, as it happens, I believe he laboured under a misapprehension, all those years, on both counts.

My own research now indicates that perhaps the immature young man of barely eighteen who left for Goodison Park in 1925 and who, by his own admission, was never one for book learning, was only prepared to believe what he wanted to believe. Being the headstrong and single-minded individual that was a major part of his genius, maybe he was unwilling or unable to accept that there are always two sides to any argument and you cannot always have things just the way you want them.

In the interests of rehabilitating the good name of Tranmere Rovers, which has been belittled all these years over these matters, I would like to put that other side and let you judge for yourself. Although there is nothing I could do, or would wish to do, to tarnish, in any way, Dixie's legendary reputation, that is not to say that we ought to allow the legend to get in the way of the facts.

Firstly, Dixie always maintained that his wages, once he had broken into the First XI in September, 1924, should have been £6.0s.0d per week. As a 17 year old who had newly turned professional in the close season, and after less than one year with a none too well off Northern Third Division club, he was paid £4.5s.0d per week. Once he had made his breakthrough into the First XI, the Football League's 1924-25 Handbook, Rule 7, made it quite clear that:

> *The maximum wage, except as hereinafter provided, shall be £5 per week, with annual rises of £1 per week to a final maximum of £6 per week during the close season, and £8 per week during the playing season. A recognised reserve team player, who by his meritorious play obtains a place in the first team, may be paid a further sum of £1 for each first team match in which he takes part.*

Dixie was, therefore, being paid the within the maximum standard starting wage for a Football League player. Thanks to the help of his nephew, Warwick Rimmer, I have been able to inspect the contract signed by Dixie's schoolboy partner, Ellis Rimmer, when he himself signed for Rovers on 12 September, 1924. He signed less than a year after Dixie had applied his own signature to a similar standard form of agreement. Written into the agreement, signed by Ellis, his father and Bert Cooke, were Ellis's contracted wages:

> *£2.5s.0d per week from 12 September, 1924, to 2 May, 1925;*
> *£4.0s.0d per week when playing for the first team;*
> *Bonus—First Team £1.0s.0d for a win, 10s.0d for a draw;*
> *Second team 10s.0d for a win, 5s.0d. for a draw.*

The idea that Dixie should have been paid £6.0s.0d a week may have stemmed from dressing room chat where the other players, all much older than himself, would have been further up the wage ladder. Given the generation (and the quality) gap between Dixie, the superb young athlete, and his under-trained, over-weight, ale-supping and cigarette smoking team-mates, well known for frequenting the Halfway House, it seems likely that Dixie was the victim of a gentle leg-pull. The evidence from Ellis Rimmer's contract makes it clear that Dixie's wages, in his first season as a professional and a First XI regular, were the going rate at £4.5s.0d per week. In fact, they were better than Ellis Rimmer's terms, reflecting, no doubt, Dixie's extra value to the club.

The second, and more serious, complaint arose when Dixie was transferred to Everton. Dixie later claimed that he had confidently expected to receive £300 as his share of the transfer fee because, so it was said, Bert Cooke had promised as much to his parents. Nevertheless, in his excitement, it was something he had failed to ask about when he signed for Everton on 16 March, 1925.

In the event, he was paid £30 and, when he was handed the cheque two weeks after the transfer, he told Bert Cooke that he had missed off a nought. He recounted to Bob Azurdia, in the 1978 Radio Merseyside interviews, that Bert replied by saying £30 was all the Football League would allow. Dixie immediately went off to see the President of the Football League, John McKenna (also chairman of Liverpool F C), but he was unable to help him.

Two incontrovertible pieces of evidence point to Dixie having entirely misunderstood his position. The first is to be found in the Birkenhead Advertiser's report of his transfer, published on 18 March, 1925:

> *..the papers have been left with Mr. John McKenna, the chairman of the Football League, to allocate the proportion (of the transfer fee) to the player. By the way, when the Rovers obtained nearly £1,000 from Stoke for Fred Groves (in 1921), the latter received £60 as his share. Dean, however, has only had a little more than one season with the Rovers.*

It is of significance because we can pinpoint how and precisely when Rovers went about establishing Dixie's share. It further indicates that time and not the size of the fee was going to be crucial in determining it. For the confirmatory piece of evidence, we need again to turn to the Football League's Handbook for 1924-25, where Rule 10 states:

> *Payment to Player in Lieu of Presumed Accrued Share of Benefit*

> *When a player is transferred, the Club transferring him may, with the consent of the Management Committee as a reward for loyal and meritorious service, pay to such a player in lieu of the amount*

which the Club has guaranteed, or would have been likely to guarantee such player for a benefit, reckoned upon the playing seasons of service in proportion to the qualifying period for a benefit with such club.

In other words, any amount the club wished to pay Dixie would have to be based on an assessment of his accrued, not his ultimate, benefit and certainly had nothing to do with the size of the transfer fee. It is also perfectly clear that Tranmere Rovers acted entirely in good faith and, at no time, sought to avoid paying Dixie his entitlement. Indeed, the very idea, that the club had somehow nefariously seduced Dixie and his parents into thinking he would be entitled to anything more, seems even less likely (although it can never be ruled out) when Rule 10 is seen to conclude with the words:

A Club, through any of its responsible officials, either promising or leading a player to hope for any payment in excess of Rule will be regarded as guilty of breach of Rule.

I now believe that, in all probability, when he first signed professional forms in the 1924 close season, Rovers had contracted to pay a benefit of £300 after ten years and Bert Cooke would have explained this to Dixie and his parents before he put pen to paper. Was Dixie, unfortunately, under the mistaken impression that he should receive the £300 on his transfer to Everton? I had hoped that Ellis Rimmer's contract would shed some light on this affair but it was frustratingly silent on the subject of benefit payments.

Having laid those two hoary old chestnuts to rest, once and for all, we must still try to understand how these circumstances might arise and forgive the very young and, later, the very old Dixie Dean for these tragic differences. Having said that, in concluding, it would only be right to recall the one grievance that we can all agree Dixie justifiably harboured.

When he joined from Pensby Institute F C in November, 1923, he asked that Rovers give them a new strip. It was on this basis that Dixie signed when he might otherwise have gone New Brighton. Despite that, it is evident that Rovers did not honour their promise and, looking back now, it seems to be the first and only good reason why Dixie took any abiding animosity towards Rovers with him to that Great Football Ground in the Sky.

If nothing else, I hope my researches have finally resolved these damaging misconceptions about Dixie's career at Prenton Park. Maybe, too, the ghost of bad times past has finally been exorcised from Prenton Park and Dixie himself will be able to look down and smile with true pleasure at the success of his first professional club!

(First published 5 & 16 May, 1990)

Birkenhead News cartoon by Glover, 3 January, 1925, v New Brighton.
Although Dixie played, he does not feature here.

CHAPTER 6

DEEP IMPRESSIONS

W hilst misunderstandings over money are nothing new, the strangest and most baffling story about Dixie's time at Prenton Park surrounds Dixie's famed injury, when still a very young man, which led to him undergoing surgery for the removal of a testicle. Obviously, this is a very sensitive topic, striking as it does at the very manhood of a justifiably proud man.

What it does not explain is why Dixie told the story the way he did and why he chose to heap the blame upon one Davy Parkes, a tough old centre half with whom he must have had a few tussles. In the light of subsequent events, one way or another, Davy must have left a deep impression on the fast maturing Dixie.

Graphically re-told in his biography by Nick Walsh and again by Dixie himself in his 1978 Radio Merseyside interviews, Dixie claimed that, in a game against Rochdale at Prenton Park, after he gave Davy Parkes the run around and scored two goals, Parkes deliberately kicked him *"where I didn't want kicking"*. He was rushed immediately to Birkenhead General Hospital where he underwent the surgery, some hours later, after the swelling went down.

Listening to that 1978 interview, you can believe that Dixie could almost still feel the pain and, at that distance of time, it made for another vivid story with which to enthral the listeners who would have been agog at such intimate revelations. Unfortunately, the facts are that it could not possibly have happened the way Dixie told it—even if he did get one thing right when he said he was out of the game for five weeks as a consequence.

During his time with Rovers, they encountered Rochdale four times, with Dixie playing in three of the games, all in the Third Division (North). He appeared twice at Spotlands, scoring just a single goal, and only once at Prenton Park, on 7 March, 1925, when he is credited with scoring a hat-trick. Within two weeks of that particular game, he was selected to make his Everton début at Highbury.

In all three games, he certainly was opposed by Davy Parkes who was clearly in the craggy mould of that Barnsley legend, Skinner Normanton. His style of defence can best be summed up by this valuable description from "R.E.T." who, with a few deft and well chosen words, has passed his unmistakable message across the years:

> *..Parkes, one of the most vigorous centre halves in the League,*
> *whose destructive work, valuable to his side, too often*
> *endangered the limbs of his opponents..*

Not only is there no report anywhere in the newspapers of any incident which remotely suggests the injury Dixie claimed was inflicted on him by Parkes, but Dixie was back in action for Rovers the following week after all three games. He did go off at half-time in the game at Rochdale, on 1 November, 1924, but that was the result of an ankle injury from a fourth minute tackle by the full-back, Stirling. Even so, Dixie still managed to carry on until half-time and score Rovers' goal in their 1-2 defeat. In the other two encounters, Dixie finished the game unscathed.

There can be no doubt that Dixie, at some time in his days at Tranmere, did suffer a traumatic experience. One that might have caused him to think that his *"matrimonial prospects"* had been permanently blighted. The only absence of five weeks which fits this story occurred in February, 1924, when he had just turned seventeen.

He played on 9 February, 1924, in the 5-3 home win over Altrincham in the Cheshire Senior Cup, scoring two goals, but did not play the following Saturday against Ellesmere Port Cement Works, in the Cheshire County League. Again, there is absolutely no evidence in the Birkenhead or the Altrincham papers of Dixie suffering such a painful injury and leaving the field. There was not the slightest hint that he was injured because he was reported in the Saturday editions of both the Birkenhead News and the Birkenhead Advertiser, on 16 February, 1924, as being down to play. The News' match report, in the mid-week edition of 20 February, 1924, merely put the absence down to Dixie being *"unwell"* but then continued, in the prospects for the next game, on 23 February, 1924:

> *The Reserve XI travel to Hurst and they will again be without Dean who is laid aside with a double rupture. All his many admirers will wish this promising boy a speedy recovery.*

Two weeks later, the News followed up on Dixie's plight when it was reported:

> *It is good to learn that Dean is not suffering from such a severe injury as was at first believed and, although he is confined to bed, he is improving nicely.*

Dixie did not play again until 15 March, 1924, when he was in the Reserve XI team against Stockport County Reserves in the Cheshire Senior Cup, scored the only goal of the game and missed a penalty. With his dry sense of humour, he was later to remind us that, when he returned, he was faster than ever now that he was *"..a stone lighter.."* - adding, *"I could sprint a bit then."*

Whilst allowing for the sensitivity of the subject which, in the mid-twenties, would no doubt have inhibited the publication of fuller details, it is perfectly evident that Dixie was not deprived of his vital organ as a result of a clash with Davy Parkes of Rochdale, or any Altrincham player for that matter. Just what did happen, we shall probably now never know.

As a postscript to this episode, during the 1978 Radio Merseyside interviews, Dixie claimed that, seventeen years afterwards, he ran into Davy Parkes in a pub in Chester and, for the only time in his life, he exacted retribution. He attacked Parkes and did him no good at all, putting him in hospital. Hopefully, the incident was as much a figment of Dixie's imagination as the original injury at Prenton Park or else poor Davy Parkes was an innocent victim.

Unless the Birkenhead and Altrincham newspapers of February, 1924, conspired to cover up any hint of Dixie's injury, one cannot help surmising that the real incident which gave rise to the surgery took place well away from Prenton Park, or any other football ground for that matter, and that Davy Parkes was the victim of Dixie's imperfect recollections over half a century after the event.

(First published 16 April, 1990)

Davy Parkes of Rochdale, the alleged cause of Dixie's "lost stone".
(Steven Phillipps)

TRANMERE ROVERS F.C. 1924-25

Birkenhead News cartoon by Glover, 11 October, 1924.

CHAPTER 7

DIXIE'S RETURN

As a postscript to the re-telling of Dixie's relationship with Tranmere Rovers, there are four further important pieces of the jigsaw.

In recent times, a belief has grown up, in the absence of any argument to the contrary, that Dixie Dean did not set foot again in Prenton Park until 45 years after his transfer to Everton in 1925. His return in 1970 for a special celebrity dinner to honour him has been held to have been the first time he came back and the build up to it reinforced the idea. It might have helped sell tickets but it is not so. Maybe the story had first started to gain credence as long ago as the early 1940s, when Dixie agreed to turn out for Rovers in a Wartime League match, on Christmas Day, 1942, against Liverpool. With player shortages, such guest appearances were very much the norm, during the war years, but there had never been a guest like this one before. An advance announcement to the public was made through the local press, creating quite a stir and a definite sense of anticipation.

Sadly, on the day, Dixie failed to turn up, without notice or explanation, much to the annoyance and embarrassment of the club and the disappointment of his fans. Was this seen as yet another reminder of past differences or was it something far less controversial arising out of the seasonal festivities and, quite simply, he preferred to be with his family? Who can tell now?

Be that as it may, he had already been back at least once. Before the War, there was a traditional end of season charity game at Prenton Park for the Birkenhead Hospitals Cup, the Egerton Laird Trophy. The game was always against attractive local opposition, the more frequent being Liverpool, and the proceeds were used to help maintain the local hospital service.

In 1934, on 2 May, it was Everton who, for the first time in many years, provided the opposition. They sent over a strong side which included Dixie and the young Joe Mercer (whose father had captained Rovers in the years immediately after the Great War). However, it was not a Dixie Dean at the height of his powers but one who had missed almost the entire 1933-34 season because of injuries and operations. He had played in only 12 of Everton's League and Cup fixtures (including the first six), scoring 9 (7) goals. The Birkenhead Hospitals Cup was the ideal kind of game at the start of his campaign to return to full fitness for the 1934-35 season.

Played before a small crowd of only 2,000, the game was not particularly exciting and Dixie was, understandably, not very active. It ended in a 3-1 win for Rovers, with the teams and scorers as follows:

ROVERS : Gray; Platt Warren: Thomas Fishwick Spencer; Pearson Watts(1) Bell(1) Glasper(1) Urmson.

EVERTON: King; Bocking Cresswell; Mercer Clark Watson; Birtley Dunn Dean Cunliffe(1) Coulter.

Rovers' own exertions had also taken their toll on them. The very next day, they had to face Bristol City in the Welsh F A Cup Final. The previous week, they had drawn 1-1 at the Racecourse, Wrexham, but in the replay, at Chester's ground in Sealand Road, Rovers were easily beaten, 0-3.

The next occasion was in 1952 when, on 25 April, Dixie was the referee of a charity game at Prenton Park between the Supporters Clubs of Rovers and New Brighton. Not exactly a high profile occasion and the report on Dixie's performance perhaps sums it up: *"Bill Dean controlled the game without moving very far from the centre circle."*

The true reconciliation took place when, on 13 January, 1970, Dixie was the chief guest at the Sportsmen's Celebrity Dinner he attended, with Joe Mercer, in Prenton Park's Vice-Presidents' Club. It was the culmination of the work of Rovers' ex-manager, Dave Russell, who has remained close to the club to this day. He knew Dixie and Joe from when he, as a Sheffield Wednesday player, played against them in the 1930s.

It was Dave Russell, soon after his appointment as manager at Prenton Park in 1961, who first extended the hand of friendship to Dixie and made him feel that Rovers had a real concern for his well-being. Dixie never had much money in his later years and Dave Russell, more than anyone, was instrumental in securing help for him from benevolent funds within the game. In the time after the amputation of his leg, in 1976, Dave also managed to persuade the Football League secretary, Alan Hardaker, to help Dixie financially. Hardaker was never an *"easy touch"* and Dave still has a sense of achievement about this.

Prior to the event, it was billed as Dixie's return, as this extract from the Liverpool Echo of 23 December, 1969, fanfares:

DEAN RETURNS TO PRENTON . . . AFTER 45 LONG YEARS

The legendary William Ralph Dean, the greatest player Tranmere Rovers—and Merseyside—have ever produced, is going back to Prenton Park for the first time since he was transferred to Everton 45 years ago. .. For reasons which are best allowed to be forgotten, in the mists of time, he has never set foot inside the ground where he started his professional career. .. Bill's photograph occupies pride of place in Tranmere's picture gallery of internationals who have been associated with the club. His record as a player and a local football genius is revered in the club—and it is good to see him going back there at last.

The evening itself was a huge success and amongst the other guests were Dave Russell and Noel Kelly (ex-Rovers' managers), Jackie Wright (Rovers' current manager), George Yardley (Rovers' current centre-forward) who was sat on Dixie's right, Kenny Campbell (ex-Liverpool), Billy Liddell (ex-Liverpool), Rovers' Chairman C.W. Hodgson and director H.A. Bainbridge. There cannot be the slightest doubt that Dixie really enjoyed himself and was thrilled when he, and Joe Mercer, were made honorary life members of the Vice-Presidents' Club. For his fellow guests and the audience, the ambience was positive and exhilarating as Dixie warmed to the unique occasion to enthral them all with his stories and memories, related in his own laconic style:

THE NIGHT DIXIE CAME HOME TO PRENTON

"I've come back" … words to crown an historic occasion last night; for they were from William Ralph Dean in the Vice-Presidents' Club at Prenton Park. And as everyone who follows football knows, the greatest centre forward of the century and Tranmere Rovers hadn't been on speaking terms for 45 years. How they came to bury the hatchet doesn't really matter. What does is that, last night at Prenton, William Ralph Dean sat as much at his ease as any man could who had a stack of menus in front of him waiting to be autographed. And a significant point—those menus were signed "Dixie Dean".

Hosts and guests at the celebrity dinner stood to acclaim him. It wasn't an emotional moment, though, rather one of complete delight. Anyway, how can you get emotional over someone who has just had you in stitches?

One of Dixie's stories was about the first goal he scored at Prenton, not for the Rovers and, indeed, not for his own side. He was playing against Liverpool Boys, promised by his father he was on a shilling if he got the ball in the net. They were four down, Dixie dropped back to "help" the defence, miskicked and that made it 5-0. Imperturbably (anyhow, that's Dixie's story) he asked for his shilling.

An exceedingly happy evening then, and the seal on it, perhaps, Dixie's own trophies on show, the illuminated address from the citizens of Birkenhead, a unique shield and his medals. All's well that ends well as this.

(Liverpool Echo, 14 January, 1970).

A happy moment. There is nothing to be added.

In November, 1979, just four months before his death, Dixie attended the Tranmere Rovers' Supporters' Association's Sports Forum as a panel member. The others were Alan Kennedy (Liverpool), Steve Coppell (Manchester United and ex-Rovers), Kevin McNally (League referee) and chairman, Brian McEvoy of the BBC. It is a fitting end to the story of Dixie and Tranmere Rovers that one of the last honours bestowed on Dixie, modest as it may seem, should have come from his first club when John Holsgrove, the Association's chairman, made him a life member.

The two events from 1934 and 1952, the role of Dave Russell leading up to the celebrity dinner in January, 1970, and the T.R.S.A. life membership granted him in 1979, ought to dispel yet another Dixie myth. They suggest that there may well have been many other occasions when Dixie returned. There can be no doubt too that, as time passed, he mellowed in his views about his old club and, in his later years, was able to enjoy himself there amongst adoring friends and fans alike.

Indeed, in his final years, Dixie was re-discovered as being a true super-star. He had never moved from Birkenhead and, so it would seem, had been taken for granted—he had always been there and he always would. He was too modest and too easy going a man to exploit his fame. Thankfully, before it was too late, he was again appreciated, even by those who did not see him at his peak, and able to enjoy once more the adulation he deserved. He was in constant demand and a delight to all who came into contact with him for his unassuming approachability and good humour.

(First published 15 January, 1991)

Birkenhead News cartoon by Glover, 16 January, 1924.
Stan Sayer, Rovers' Leading Marksman.

CHAPTER 8

ROVERS' YOUNGEST—DEAN OR DEMPSEY?

F ollowing my series of articles last season about Dixie Dean's career at Prenton Park, my attention was recently drawn to some contradictory evidence about Dixie's claim to have been the youngest player to appear for Rovers in the Football League.

In the Birkenhead News & Advertiser of Wednesday, 1 May, 1968, Stuart Hooton, their much respected and well informed correspondent on Rovers' affairs in the 1950s and 1960s, claimed that particular distinction for full-back John W Dempsey. John made his Football League début, in the penultimate game of the season, at Bournemouth on 2 May, 1968, and Stuart Hooton wrote:

DEMPSEY SETS A DEBUT RECORD.

Six months ago, the name of John Dempsey was unknown, even in the Cheshire League. Hardly surprising—for when he made his début for Tranmere Rovers against Runcorn on October 6th, he was a mere sixteen and a half, and had been an apprentice for only a few weeks.

Tomorrow, one month after his 17th birthday, he is thrust into first-team football and plays for Rovers at left-back. This makes him the youngest player ever to wear Rovers' colours in a Football League game. He is still an apprentice, and his second-team experience amounts to 20 games.

Although no taller than most 17-year-olds, Dempsey is solidly built, and weighs more than 11 stone. Manager Dave Russell says: "He's strong, and has made good progress." Those who watch the Reserves will agree. I saw the second team play Rhyl on Tuesday night, and was highly impressed with Dempsey's performance. He looked the outstanding prospect.

This is a remarkably surprising claim for Stuart Hooton to have made given his depth of knowledge about the club's history and players. Whilst he was extremely well informed from first hand knowledge of post-War events, he would also have learned about earlier times from the then still active chronicler of Rovers' doings from 1912 onwards, R E (Eric) Thompson, or "R.E.T."

John Dempsey was indeed 17 years and one month, having been born on 2 April, 1951, when he turned out at Bournemouth but Dixie was only 16 years 355 days when he made his Football League début at inside right at Rotherham on 12 January, 1924. There can be no doubt that to Dixie remains the distinction of being Rovers' youngest ever Football League débutant.

In the Tranmere Rovers Official Yearbook, published prior to the 1968-69 season, the claim for John Dempsey was repeated. The confusion was compounded as it referred to John's debut having been made at Brentford, even though they were in the Fourth Division at the time while Rovers were in the Third!

Despite the early promise, John Dempsey's own career with Rovers was to end in 1971-72 season, after making 52 appearances plus 3 substitute appearances and scoring one goal.

(First published 18 March, 1991)

John Dempsey

CHAPTER 9

STAN SAYER—PAST MASTER 1923-1925

There he is, in that historic 1924-25 team photograph, sat sitting next to the greatest player of them all, the young and undeniably so gifted Dixie Dean. Usually portrayed, a trifle unfairly, by the Birkenhead News' cartoonist, Glover, as being a portly figure of a man, he seemed to be the very antithesis of the superb athlete sat on his immediate right. His own career was now on the wane and the seventeen year old Dixie was about to burst onto the world. What a difference! But perhaps it was not all bad news. He was about to play his own small, yet crucial, role in soccer history.

Stanley Charles Sayer had just turned 28 when, on 15 March, 1923, he signed for Rovers from Millwall for a fee of £25. Very much a novelty in those days, he was a Southerner, born in Chatham on 2 February, 1895, who now found himself far from home in the distant, you might say alien, pastures of Merseyside and the Northern Section of the Third Division. For the past year or so he had been in dispute with Millwall over his contract and Millwall had put an exaggerated transfer fee on his head. When this happened, Stan took himself off to play non-League football for Northfleet, a team from Kent, until Millwall, forced to relent by the Football League, allowed him to join Rovers. Rovers' League position was not very good at the time of Stan's arrival, being third from bottom, although they had improved matters somewhat since January when they had actually been at the foot at the table.

Having spent his pre-Millwall career up to 1921 in Army football and with Ramsgate Town, Stan was 5 feet 8 inches tall, weighed 11 stone 6 pounds and was a skilful and effective inside right or centre forward—a striker in today's language. He made his immediate début against Wrexham at the Racecourse on 17 March, 1923, scoring Rovers' only goal, with a powerful shot, in a 1-2 defeat in front of 6,250 spectators. He created a favourable impression with his ability to keep the ball low and his harassing of the home defence, never allowing them to make a clearance unchallenged. Rovers' team in his Racecourse début was:

> Bradshaw; Thompson Stuart; Campbell Halstead Sewell;
> Moreton Sayer Crowther Lomax Evans.

In the return game the following week, the popular Sammy Beswick, whom Stan had displaced, replaced the hapless Crowther for the rest of the season.

He went on to score eight more goals in Rovers' remaining seven League games of 1922-23 season to help them to the relative respectability of being five places off the bottom. He also achieved the rare and unexpected distinction of being Tranmere's top scorer for the season (one more than Beswick) after just eight games! He also contributed another couple of goals in Liverpool Senior Cup and Cheshire Senior Medals games.

Season 1923-24 saw Stan establish himself as the club's number one goalscorer as Rovers enjoyed their best season since joining the Football League in 1921, finishing a comfortable mid-table twelfth. He missed just one of the 42 League games that season and scored sixteen goals in the process, again ending up as top scorer, ahead of Jack Brown and Harry Littlehales, who each managed only eight. He was regarded as the natural hero of the forward line but his general play was also of a quality that drew the appreciation of the Prenton Park faithful.

He was the intelligent kind of player who was unselfish and contributed to a more cohesive style of team play by his willingness and ability to bring his inside forwards into play and also to spread the ball to the wings where Jimmy Moreton, on the right, and Bert Cartman, a close season signing from Manchester United, on the left, had the ability to take on men and get in telling crosses. Perhaps these two plaudits from the Rochdale Observer in 1924 tell us something about Stan's brainy play:

> *Sayer is a clever centre-forward and dangerous when given a little scope, but Parkes watched him well and acquitted himself well generally.*

> *Sayer was always an elusive player to mark...*

The highlight of the season for Stan was, unquestionably, his winning hat-trick in 5th Qualifying Road of the F A Cup (today's equivalent of Round 2) against Coventry City of the Second Division. The first game was away, on 1 December, 1923, (the day Dixie made his Second XI début) and, before a large crowd of 13,352 (gate receipts £755), Rovers forced a 2-2 draw with goals from Irish international, Jack Brown. In the replay, the following Thursday afternoon (Birkenhead's traditional half day closing), despite losing pivot Fred Halstead for 40 minutes with a head injury, 6,000 Roverites saw Stan twice put Rovers in the lead before City equalised for the second time with just four minutes to go. Seven minutes into extra time, the crowd went wild when Stan headed in Jimmy Moreton's cross to take a 3-2 lead which is where it stood when the game finished. It seemed that all Stan's skills in working with his wingers and inside men came good this particular day to clinch a famous victory but one which was not to be repeated in the next round, away to non-League Gillingham, where Rovers went down 0-1.

Season 1924-25 saw Stan the goalscorer inevitably overshadowed by the extraordinary exploits of Dixie Dean who was to score 27 League goals in 27 games before his transfer to Everton in March, 1925. In his 29 games, Stan could muster just five goals (plus one in the F A Cup) but Stan the goaltaker had become Stan the goalmaker as he encouraged Dixie's rampages through the terror stricken defences of the Northern Section from Accrington to Ashington, Barrow to Bradford, Halifax to Hartlepools, Rochdale to Rotherham and Walsall to Wigan.

It was in no small measure down to Stan Sayer, who was operating as a right half in Dixie's last three games, that the constant cry ringing round Prenton Park became *"Give it to Dixie!"* And Stan, with his shrewd and experienced footballing brain, knew this was exactly what he and his colleagues had to do. When, on 15 November, 1924, Stan was featured in the match programme's personality feature, *"The Personal Touch"*, this was the inside view of his contribution:

> *Owing to the promising form being shown by "Dixie" Dean, it was deemed advisable, in order to allow for his inclusion in the first team, to move Stan Sayer from the centre berth to inside-right, soon after the season started. Seeing that the popular Londoner was last campaign our leading marksman, with sixteen goals, there were some who thought the change would affect his play, but experience has proved the reverse to be the case. Stan has been a source of delight, week in and week out, as a result of his artistic display, and there is no doubt his judicious work has been an important factor in the rapid rise to fame of our boy leader. Stan, it is true, has thus far only found the net once, but most of the goals obtained by us thus far have been the outcome of his scheming. The secret of his success is that he uses his brains and makes the ball do the work all the time.*

If Barry Dyson had his Dave Hickson, if Keith Williams had his Tony Rowley, if Harold Atkinson had his Bill Bainbridge, if Ian Muir has his Jim Steel, then I believe it can be said that Dixie had his Stan Sayer. Maybe they were at different ends of their chosen career paths, maybe Stan, like so many of his team-mates, preferred his Halfway House pint and his fags to Dixie's dedication to skills and fitness, maybe one was a Northerner and one was a Southerner, but somehow they gelled for those few heady months as a giant nova star became visible and began its spectacular progress across the soccer firmament of the twenties and thirties.

If we were to be offered a once only opportunity to take a time machine trip and go back to watch Rovers of times past, surely that would have to be the choice of us all and wouldn't Prenton Park be packed to the rafters to catch a just a glimpse of the *"talented boy leader"* that was Dixie? And there beside him, prompting him at every opportunity, would be Stan Sayer.

But back to Stan's own career. In the 1925 close season, on 8 July, he too moved on and also just "down the road", as it were, but in his case to the far less glamourous precincts of Sandheys Park, New Brighton. He never settled there (12 appearances and 5 goals) and quickly moved on to Wigan Borough (November, 1925), Lincoln City (March, 1926), Southend United (July, 1927) and, finally, Dartford in 1929. This seems a dismal end to the career of a player who was considered "brainy" and had shown such style in his play.

43

What he did after he quit football I have not been able to discover but you can bet your life that he spent the next fifty-odd years, until he died, at the ripe old age of 87, on 5 April, 1982, in Westbourne, Dorset, telling the regulars down at his local how he had been the Master and Dixie Dean had been his star pupil. His aggregate record when with Tranmere Rovers was:

	LEAGUE		F A CUP		TOTAL	
	A	**G**	**A**	**G**	**A**	**G**
1922-23	8	9	0	0	8	9
1923-24	41	16	4	3	45	19
1924-25	29	5	4	1	33	6
TOTALS	**78**	**30**	**8**	**4**	**86**	**34**

(First published 5 & 8 November, 1991, in the Past Masters series)

Stan Sayer as seen by the Liverpool Echo's George Green.

New Brighton's "Bert" Mehaffy clears from Stan Sayer during the game at Prenton Park on 13 October, 1923. Stan scored Rovers' goal in the 1-2 defeat.

(Peter Bishop)

45

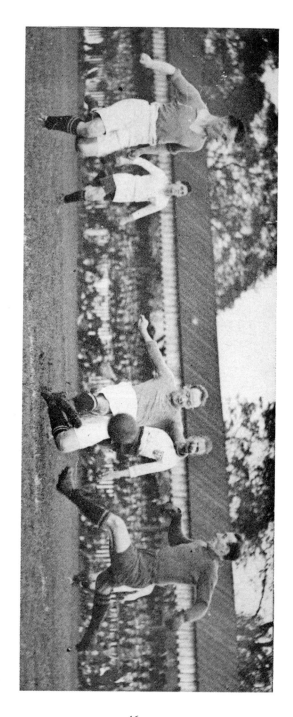

Another clash between Stan and Mehaffy. The original caption relates that both were injured as a result. The other Rovers player in view is Irish International Jack Brown.

(Peter Bishop)

46

Stan Sayer scoring the winner against Grimsby Town in the opening game of
1923-24 season (25 August). The terrace in the background is now the site of the main stand.

(Peter Bishop)

Stan Sayer (second from right) beats Southport 'keeper, Halsall, in the 1-1 draw on 8 September, 1923. The terrace in the background backs onto Borough Road.

(Peter Bishop)

Dixie's Return to Prenton Park, 13 January, 1970. Dixie shares a glass and a moment of sheer enjoyment with his good friend, young Joe Mercer.

(Liverpool Echo & Daily Post)

Dixie's Return—he is flanked by (L-R) Dave Russell, Kenny Campbell, Noel Kelly, Joe Mercer, Billy Liddell, George Yardley and Jackie Wright. Dixie's relaxed and happy mood is apparent to all.

(Liverpool Echo & Daily Post)

Admiring the new "team bus", Rovers squad, with Bert Cooke in characteristic pose, prepares for an away trip with an over-inflated ball!! Heaven only knows what was going on here. Probably taken prior to season 1925-26, after Dixie's departure.

(Ron Kennedy)

The Annual Prenton Park Gurning Competition with "Ginger" Lewis the outright winner!! Also, circa 1925-26.

(Ron Kennedy)

APPENDIX A

CHRONOLOGY OF DIXIE DEAN'S GAMES 1923-24

DATE	OPPONENTS	COMP	V	F-A	GOALS
1923					
1 December	Whitchurch	CCL	H	1-3	1 Tranmere Rovers début
8 December	Hurst	CCL	H	4-1	1
15 December	Frodsham	CSC	H	8-1	3
22 December	Winsford United	CCL	A	1-2	1
25 December	Wallasey United	CCL	A	1-2	
26 December	Wallasey United	CCL	H	3-2	1
29 December	Ashton National	CCL	A	1-1	1 Penalty
1924					
1 January	Ellesmere Port Cement Works	CCL	A	1-3	
5 January	Port Vale Reserves	CCL	A	1-3	
9 January	New Brighton	LSC	A	4-2	1 First XI début
12 January	Rotherham County	3N	A	1-5	Football League début
19 January	Ashton National	CCL	A	1-3	
26 January	Nantwich	CCL	H	5-2	3 (1 penalty)
2 February	Congleton Town	CCL	A	1-1	1 Penalty
9 February	Altrincham	CSC	H	5-3	2
16 February	Ellesmere Port C W	CCL	H	3-3	⎫
23 February	Hurst	CCL	A	1-6	⎬ Injured—did
1 March	Congleton Town	CCL	H	2-1	not play
8 March	Chester Reserves	CCL	A	Off	⎭
15 March	Stockport County Reserves	CSC	H	1-0	1
22 March	Crewe Alexandra Reserves	CCL	A	1-4	
29 March	Winsford United	CCL	H	2-1	1
2 April	Northwich Victoria	CCL	A	0-4	
5 April	Nantwich	CCL	A	1-2	Missed a penalty
7 April	Witton Albion	CCL	H	2-0	1
12 April	Chester Reserves	CCL	H	0-0	
14 April	Stockport County Reserves	CCL	H	1-2	
19 April	Sandbach Ramblers	CCL	A	0-3	
21 April	New Brighton Reserves	CSC	H	0-0	Final
22 April	Rochdale	3N	A	0-1	
26 April	Chester Reserves	CCL	A	2-3	1
29 April	Port Vale Reserves	CCL	H	2-5	
1 May	Middlewich	CCL	H	7-0	5 (Rimmer 2)
3 May	Wolverhampton Wanderers	3N	H	0-0	
7 May	New Brighton Reserves	CSC	A	0-1	Final replay

	3N	CCL	CSC	LSC	TOTAL
Appearances	3	22	5	1	31
Goals	0	17	6	1	24

3N   Football League Division 3 (North)
CCL   Cheshire County League
CSC   Cheshire Senior Cup
LSC   Liverpool Senior Cup

CHRONOLOGY OF DIXIE DEAN'S GAMES 1924-25

DATE	OPPONENTS	COMP	V	F-A	GOALS	
1924						
16 August	BLUES v Reds	PS	H	1-3	1	
19 August	REDS v Blues	PS	H	5-3	3	
23 August	REDS v Blues	PS	H	7-5	2	
30 August	Port Vale Reserves	CCL	H	1-2		
3 September	Nantwich	CCL	A	4-2	4	
6 September	Stalybridge Celtic	CCL	A	0-3		Injured—did not play
11 September	Whitchurch	CCL	H	7-2	5	
13 September	Doncaster Rovers	3N	A	0-2		
15 September	Witton Albion	CCL	A	2-0		
20 September	Southport	3N	H	1-0	1	First Football League goal
25 September	Crewe Alexandra	CSM	H	4-1	1	
27 September	Ashington	3N	A	0-1		
2 October	Walsall	3N	H	0-1		
4 October	Nelson	3N	H	2-0	1	
11 October	Barrow	3N	A	1-1	1	
18 October	Lincoln City	3N	A	2-3	2	
25 October	Hartlepools United	3N	H	4-3	3	
1 November	Rochdale	3N	A	1-2	1	Ankle injury, missed
8 November	Darlington	3N	H	0-1		second half
15 November	Crewe Alexandra	FAC	H	1-1		Injured, did not play
19 November	Crewe Alexandra	FAC	A	2-0		Replay
22 November	Wrexham	3N	H	2-0		
29 November	Southport	FAC	H	1-1		
3 December	Southport	FAC	A	0-1		Replay
6 December	Chesterfield	3N	H	5-1	2	
13 December	Stockport County	CSM	A	0-2		Final
20 December	Halifax Town	3N	A	3-1	2	
25 December	Bolton Wanderers Reserves	Frly	H	1-2		Did not play
26 December	New Brighton	3N	A	0-1		
27 December	Crewe Alexandra	3N	H	2-2	2	
1925						
1 January	New Brighton	3N	H	1-3	1	
3 January	Durham City	3N	A			Postponed
10 January	Walsall	3N	A		0-2	Injured—missed 2nd half
17 January	Doncaster Rovers	3N	H	1-2		
24 January	Southport	3N	A	0-1		
31 January	Ashington	3N	H	5-4	2	
7 February	Nelson	3N	A	1-4	1	
14 February	Barrow	3N	H	4-1	3	
21 February	Lincoln City	3N	H	0-0		
28 February	Hartlepools United	3N	A	1-2	1	
4 March	Bradford Park Avenue	3N	A	1-5		
7 March	Rochdale	3N	H	3-1	3	
14 March	Darlington	3N	A	1-2	1	Injured—missed last 20 minutes

	3N	FAC	CCL	CSM	PS	TOTAL
Appearances	27	3	4	2	3	39
Goals	27	0	9	1	6	43

3N Football League Division 3 (North)
FAC Football Association Challenge Cup
CCL Cheshire County League
CSM Cheshire Senior Medals
PS Pre-season public trial game

APPENDIX C

DIXIE DEAN'S FIRST XI TEAMS 1924-25

FOOTBALL LEAGUE—DIVISION 3 (NORTH)

1924

13 September	Doncaster Rovers (a) 0-2	Mitchell; G Jackson Stuart; Campbell Halstead Griffiths; Moreton Brown Dean Littlehales Rimmer.
20 September	Southport (h) 1-0	Mitchell; G Jackson Stuart; Crewe Halstead Campbell; Moreton Sayer Dean(1) Littlehales Cartman.
27 September	Ashington (a) 0-1	Mitchell; G Jackson Stuart; Crewe Halstead Campbell; Moreton Sayer Dean Cartman Rimmer.
2 October	Walsall (h) 0-1	Briggs; G Jackson Stuart; Crewe Halstead Campbell; Moreton Sayer Dean Cartman Griffiths.
4 October	Nelson (h) 2-0	Briggs; G Jackson Stuart; Crewe Halstead Campbell; Moreton(1) Sayer Dean(1) Cartman Griffiths.
11 October	Barrow (a) 1-1	Mitchell; G Jackson Stuart; Crewe Halstead Campbell; Moreton Sayer Dean(1) Cartman Griffiths.
18 October	Lincoln City (a) 2-3	Mitchell; G Jackson Stuart; Crewe Halstead Campbell; Birtles Sayer Dean(2) Cartman Griffiths.
25 October	Hartlepools United (h) 4-3	Mitchell; G Jackson Stuart; Checkland Halstead Campbell; Cartman Sayer(1) Dean(3) Brown Rimmer.
1 November	Rochdale (a) 1-2	Mitchell; G Jackson Stuart; Crewe Halstead Campbell; Moreton Sayer Dean(1) Brown Cartman.
8 November	Darlington (h) 0-1	Mitchell; G Jackson Stuart; Crewe Halstead Campbell; Moreton Sayer Dean Rothwell Cartman.
22 November	Wrexham (h) 2-0	Mitchell; G Jackson Stuart(1); Jeffs Halstead Campbell; Moreton Sayer Dean Littlehales(1) Cartman.
6 December	Chesterfield (h) 5-1	Mitchell; Stuart Naylor; Crewe Jeffs Rutter; Moreton Brown(1) Dean(2) Littlehales(2) Cartman.
20 December	Halifax Town (a) 3-1	Briggs; Stuart Naylor; Jeffs Halstead Rutter; Moreton Brown Dean(2) Sayer(1) Cartman.

55

26 December	New Brighton	Briggs; G Jackson Stuart; Jeffs
	(a) 0-1	Halstead Rutter; Moreton Brown Dean
		Sayer Cartman.

27 December	Crewe Alexandra	Briggs; G Jackson Naylor; Jeffs
	(h) 2-2	Halstead Rutter; Moreton Brown Dean(2)
		Sayer Cartman.

1925

1 January	New Brighton	Briggs; G Jackson Stuart; Jeffs
	(h) 1-3	Halstead Rutter; Moreton Brown Dean(1)
		Sayer Cartman.

10 January	Walsall	Briggs; G Jackson Stuart; Crewe
	(a) 0-2	Jeffs Rutter; Moreton Sayer Dean
		Rothwell Cartman.

17 January	Doncaster Rovers	Briggs; Stuart Naylor; Crewe
	(h) 1-2	Jeffs Rutter; Cartman Sayer Dean
		Littlehales(1) Griffiths.

24 January	Southport	Briggs; Crewe Stuart; Jeffs
	(a) 0-1	Halstead Rutter; Cartman Sayer Dean
		Littlehales Griffiths.

31 January	Ashington	Briggs; Crewe Stuart; Jeffs
	(h) 5-4	Halstead Rutter; Cartman Fogg(1) Dean(2)
		Littlehales(2) Rimmer.

7 February	Nelson	Briggs; G Jackson Stuart; Crewe
	(a) 1-4	Halstead Checkland; Cartman Fogg Dean(1)
		Littlehales Rimmer.

14 February	Barrow	Briggs; G Jackson Stuart; Checkland
	(h) 4-1	Halstead Rutter; Cartman Fogg(1) Dean(3)
		Sayer Rimmer.

21 February	Lincoln City	Briggs; G Jackson Stuart; Checkland
	(h) 0-0	Halstead Rutter; Cartman Fogg Dean
		Littlehales Rimmer.

28 February	Hartlepools United	Briggs; G Jackson Stuart; Checkland
	(a) 1-2	Halstead Crewe; Cartman Fogg Dean(1)
		Littlehales Rimmer.

4 March	Bradford Park Avenue	Briggs; G Jackson Stuart; Sayer
	(a) 1-5	Halstead Checkland; Cartman Brown Dean
		Littlehales(1) Rimmer.

7 March	Rochdale	Briggs; G Jackson Stuart; Sayer
	(h) 3-1	Jeffs Rutter; Cartman Brown Dean(3)
		Littlehales Rimmer.

14 March	Darlington	Briggs; Lewis Stuart; Sayer
	(a) 1-2	Halstead Rutter; Cartman Brown Dean(1)
		Littlehales Rimmer.

FOOTBALL ASSOCIATION CHALLENGE CUP

1924

19 November	Crewe Alexandra	Mitchell; G Jackson Stuart; Jeffs
	QR 4 Replay	Halstead Campbell(1); Moreton Sayer Dean
	(a) 2-0	Littlehales(1) Cartman.
29 November	Southport	Mitchell; G Jackson Stuart; Crewe
	QR 5	Halstead Campbell; Cartman Sayer(1) Dean
	(h) 1-1	Littlehales Evans.
3 December	Southport	Mitchell; G Jackson Stuart; Checkland
	QR 5 Replay	Halstead Rutter; Birtles Sayer Dean
	(a) 0-1	Littlehales Cartman.

CHESHIRE SENIOR MEDALS

1924

25 September	Crewe Alexandra	Mitchell; G Jackson Stuart; Crewe
		Halstead Campbell; Cartman Sayer(1) Dean(1)
	(h) 4-1	Rothwell(2) Rimmer.
13 December	Stockport County	Mitchell; Stuart Naylor;
	Final	Crewe Jeffs Rutter;
	(a) 0-2	Moreton Brown Dean Sayer Cartman.

∞

DIXIE DEAN'S FULL RECORD AT TRANMERE ROVERS

NOVEMBER 1923 TO MARCH 1925

	3N	FAC	CCL	CSC	CSM	LSC	PS	TOTAL
Appearances	30	3	26	5	2	1	3	70
Goals	27	0	26	6	1	1	6	67

3N	Football League Division 3 (North)
FAC	Football Association Challenge Cup
CCL	Cheshire County League
CSC	Cheshire Senior Cup
CSM	Cheshire Senior Medals
LSC	Liverpool Senior Cup
PS	Pre-season public trial game.

FOOTNOTE: It was first pointed out by Phil Thompson in his book, "The Fabulous Dixie", published in Autumn, 1990, that Dixie appeared in three Football League games in 1923 - 24 season, not two. Even career details published in the 1930s, during his days at Everton, had, until this was discovered by Phil Thompson, been understated. Strangely, I was aware of the Rotherham and Rochdale games but not the Wolves one; Phil Thompson identified the Rochdale game down as the one newly discovered.

Dixie as pictured in R.E.T.'s article about his transfer to Everton.
(Birkenhead News)

SELECTED FULL REPORTS FROM LOCAL NEWSPAPERS 1924-25

MORE ABOUT DEAN

(By "R.E.T.")

In case there is more ink spilled in certain quarters, I take this the earliest opportunity of giving the latest details about the Rovers and Dixie Dean. On Wednesday last, Mr. Bert Cooke was at Goodison Park for the purpose of witnessing the international match between England and Ireland, which by the way the home country won by 3-1, and during the course of the game he was approached by representatives of several of the leading clubs in the land. All had the same mission making enquiry as to what the Rovers wanted for the talented boy leader Dean. The reply given to all was the same, "There is nothing doing. Dean is not on offer."

The answer greatly upset one of the missionaries who from his attitude suggested that he had a big cheque ready for business. Mr. Cooke could not fail to notice it, and at the conclusion of the game he drew the disappointed one into a room and the individual in question evidently thought he was moving in the right way, as his face lit up. All he was told, however, was, "Seeing that it is your club, the Rovers might consider if the offer is big enough letting you have a photo of Dean!"

(Birkenhead News, Saturday, 25 October, 1924)

∽✕∾

DEAN'S DEPARTURE.

Transferred to Everton at Record Fee.

(By "R.E.T.")

While it was generally felt that Tranmere Rovers would sooner or later part company with their youthful talented leader, W. R. (Dixie) Dean, the fact remains that the official announcement of his transfer to Everton on Monday has come as a severe blow to the more ardent supporters of the local club.

The deal was completed at the Woodside Hotel on Monday evening, and I can with authority state that the figure obtained was, as near as makes no matter, £3,000. This, of course, is a record figure paid for a player who is only 19 (sic) years of age, and moreover stands as the highest sum expended on any player connected with Third Division football. As a result the Rovers are in the happy position of being free from debt so far as the working of the club is concerned— there is still the ground debt—and the directors have rid themselves of what has been a nightmare standing as they have been for some seasons as guarantors for a bank overdraft of close upon £3,000.

Looking at the matter from the ordinary enthusiast's point of view, the departure of Dean is to be regretted, and it cannot be gainsaid that the Birkenhead boy by his play and scoring feats has been the main draw at Prenton Park all this season. Dean has done well in a side that has fared badly, and now that he has gone I personally believe that the gates will suffer, particularly as he has gone to a club in the vicinity and within easy access of all his admirers, who will not unnaturally be keen to see for themselves how he progresses with the "Toffies".

Many are asking how the Rovers can hope to rise to higher spheres if the club parts with really promising young players, and of course this is a rather pointed question. The pity of it is that the responsibility comes back upon the public, for had the Rovers been given support more in keeping with a town the size of Birkenhead things might have been different. No one more regrets the passing from the Rovers of Dean than I do, but one must not be too ready in face of all the facts to hurl abuse at the directorate.

The first point is that Dean has taken up professional football as his livelihood, and in this direction it would have been grossly unfair for the Rovers to have barred the way up and from taking a step up the ladder of fame when the opportunity came. Dixie is a born and natural footballer, and if he steers clear of injury I believe he will achieve the highest honours the game has to bestow upon him. Then again the directors had their own position to consider, and no one can blame them for relieving themselves of a threatening financial situation.

This is taking the broad view, and it only remains for me to join in wishing Dean the best of luck in his new sphere, and that he will continue to develop on the same lines he has shown since he first became associated with the Rovers.

(Birkenhead News, Wednesday, 18 March, 1925)

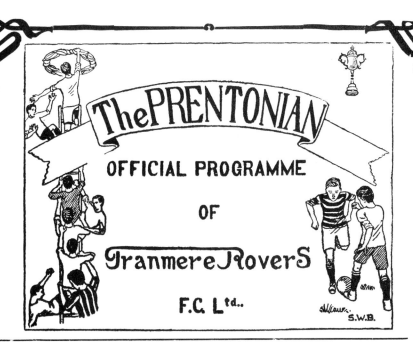

ThePRENTONIAN

OFFICIAL PROGRAMME
OF
Tranmere Rovers
F.C. L^{td}..

S.W.B.

| No. 28 | SATURDAY, MARCH 7th, 1925. | Price Twopence |

YATES'
ALES

ALWAYS IN SPLENDID
CONDITION & FLAVOUR

PRINTED BY WILSON & JONES, 92 HAMILTON ST., BIRKENHEAD

Tranmere Rovers v Rochdale, 7 March, 1925—match programme.
Dixie's last home game for Rovers and the only occasion he faced Davy Parkes
at Prenton Park. Two weeks later he made his Everton début at Highbury.
(George Higham)

Editorial Musings.

THE ODD GOAL AGAIN.

Although the journey, on Saturday last, to West Hartlepool was made under more comfortable circumstances than was the case last campaign, when the long route to the north-east was made by road, it so turned out that the result was identical—a defeat for us by the odd goal in three. This was the tenth occasion this season that our boys have met with an odd goal reverse, and while it is some satisfaction that very few clubs in the Northern Section, thus far, have demonstrated any real superiority over us, still, the fact remains, that we continue to hover in the lower regions of the chart. The United's ground was in a very good condition, and the game on the whole was of an interesting character. In three minutes the home men scored, but where kept in check thereafter, although the point obtained sufficed to give them the lead at the change of ends. In the second half our boys revealed much better form, and once again Dixie Dean demonstrated his cleverness by

scoring a really brilliant goal. Gaining possession in midfield he outwitted three opponents before delivering a smashing drive that flashed into the net at great pace. It was a typical Dean effort, and the home supporters gave the effort the unstinted applause it merited. The subsequent play ruled on fairly even lines, and just when everything pointed to a draw the home then obtained a further goal five minutes from time.

RESERVES EASY WIN.

Our Reserve eleven gained a comfortable victory over Runcorn by four clear goals, and once again claim the honour of having scored more goals than any other side in the Cheshire County League. Our debutant, Critchlow, who formerly played with West Kirby, had unfavourable conditions for a try-out, but put up quite a promising show.

. The .
REGENT
CHURCH RD., TRANMERE (3 minutes from ground)

Continuous from 6-30, except Saturdays and Bank Holiday, then two separate performances at 6-30 & 8-40

Rovers' Fixtures and Results for 1924-25.

ENGLISH LEAGUE—DIV. III.

1923-24 RESULT F. A.	DATE	OPPONENTS	GR'ND	RESULT F. A.
1 1	1924 Aug. 30—Crewe Alexandra		A	2 0
1 5	Sept. 1—Rotherham		A	0 2
1 0	6—Durham City		H	1 1
1 1	13—Doncaster R.		A	1 0
8 3	20—Southport		H	0 1
3 1	27—Ashington		A	0 1
	Oct. 2—Walsall		H	2 0
1 1	4—Nelson		A	1 1
1 1	11—Barrow		H	2 3
8 0	18—Lincoln City		A	4 3
1 1	25—Hartlepools		H	1 2
0 0	Nov. 1—Rochdale		A	2 0
1 4	8—Darlington		H	1 3
	22—Wrexham		A	1 1
	29—Southport (F.A. Cup—5th Qual. Round)		H	0 1
	Dec. 3—Southport (F.A. Cup—replay)		A	5 1
0 0	6—Chesterfield		h	0 2
	13—Stockport (Cheshire Medals)		A	3 1
0 0	20—Halifax		A	1 3
	25—Bolton Wanderers Res. (Friendly)		H	0 1
0 0	26—New Brighton		A	2 1
1 1	27—Crewe Alexandra		H	0 8
1 2	Jan. 1—New Brighton		H	1 2
	10—Walsall		A	0 1
4 0	17—Doncaster R.		H	1 2
3 0	24—Southport		A	0 1
1 1	31—Ashington		H	5 4
2 4	Feb. 7—Nelson		A	1 1
	14—Barrow		A	4 1
3 0	21—Lincoln City		H	0 7
1 3	28—Hartlepools		A	1 2
1 2	Bradford			
2 1	Mar. 7—Rochdale		H	
2 1	14—Darlington		A	
	16—			
2 1	21—Bradford		H	
1 1	28—Wrexham		H	
0 1	April 4—Rotherham		H	
2 1	10—Grimsby		A	
5 0	11—Chesterfield		A	
0 0	13—Grimsby Town		H	
6 0	14—Wigan		A	
2 0	18—Accrington		A	
3 0	25—Halifax		H	
2	May 2—Wigan Borough		A	

CHESHIRE COUNTY LEAGUE.

923-24 RESULT F. A.	DATE	OPPONENTS	GR'ND	RESULT F. A.
	1924 Aug. 30—Port Vale		H	1 2
2 5	Sept. 3—Nantwich		A	4 2
1 2	6—Stalybridge		H	0 1
0 4	11—Whitchurch		H	7 2
1 3	13—Manchester N.E.		H	3 4
	15—Witton		A	2 0
1 3	20—Port Vale		A	1 2
4 0	27—Macclesfield		H	2 0
1 1	Oct. 4—Congleton		A	3 3
0 2	11—Sandbach		H	5 1
	18—Stalybridge		H	3 0
	25—Ellesmere Port T.		A	3 1
1 1	Nov. 1—Ashton		H	2 3
1 3	8—Whitchurch		A	2 3
1 2	15—Runcorn		A	0 2
	22—Altrincham		H	2 0
	29—			
1 2	Dec. 6—Macclesfield		A	2 1
4 2	13—Altrincham		A	4 2
	20—Ashton Bros. 1st Round Ches. S. Cup		H	7 0
2 0	25—Crewe		A	2 2
1 4	26—Chester		A	2 3
1 2	27—Winsford		A	2 2
2 1	Jan. 1—Northwich		A	1 10
	3—Northwich		H	5 1
	10—Winsford		H	5 3
	17—Crewe (2nd Round Ches. S. Cup)		A	3 6
3 0	24—Mossley		H	1 3
	31—Manchester N.E.		A	1 1
0 0	Feb. 7—Middlewich		H	3 1
1 2	14—Ashton		A	1 6
1 3	21—Hurst		H	4 0
2 2	28—Runcorn		H	
2 5	Mar. 7—Mossley		A	
0 0	14—Chester		H	
2 1	28—Congleton		H	
	April 4—			
1 4	10—Ellesmere Port C.		A	
3 3	11—Ellesmere Port C.		H	
2 2	25—Nantwich		H	
4 1	25—Middlewich		A	
	30—Hurst		A	
3 3	May 2—Crewe		A	

63

LEAGUE—DIVISION 3 (Northern). COMPLETE CHART OF RESULTS, 1924-25

Home Teams \ Visitors	Accrington	Ashington	Barrow	Bradford	Chesterfield	Crewe	Darlington	Doncaster R.	Durham	Grimsby	Halifax	Hartlepool	Lincoln	Nelson	New Brighton	Rochdale	Rotherham C	Southport	Tranmere	Walsall	Wigan	Wrexham
Accrington		2-2	1-2	2-2	2-2		2-0			0-3	2-0	4-1		2-0		2-2	2-0	5-1			3-1	
Ashington	1-2		5-2		2-1	1-1	4-2	2-0		0-3	2-1	1-1	1-1	4-3	3-1				1-0	6-1	1-1	2-0
Barrow	3-1	3-2			1-0	2-0	0-4	4-0	2-0		2-1	1-1	1-2	3-0	1-1				1-0	1-1	3-2	2-2
Bradford	3-0	7-1	1-1			6-1		4-1	4-7	0-1	2-1	3-0		5-2	0-0	3-0			5-1		2-2	3-0
Chesterfield	1-0	1-1				1-0	0-1	2-1		1-3	4-0		0-1	3-0	2-0		1-2			1-0	3-1	3-0
Crewe	4-2	1-0	3-1	2-1			0-5	1-1	3-0				3-1	1-1	1-0	2-0	3-1	1-1	0-2	1-1	1-1	
Darlington			2-1		3-3	5-1			0-0	0-0	3-0	2-0	0-1	3-1	3-1	2-0	4-0	2-1		3-0	5-0	3-1
Doncaster R.	4-1	7-3	0-0	1-0		1-1	0-2			0-0	1-0	2-1	1-0		4-1			2-0	2-1	5-0	1-0	
Durham		0-0	1-0	1-1	4-1		1-0			6-1	1-2	5-0			3-2	0-0			0-2		1-1	1-0
Grimsby	4-0	1-3	2-1	2-0	0-0	0-0	0-2		1-1			1-1	2-1	1-2	2-2	1-1	3-1		2-1		0-1	
Halifax	2-2	3-0	2-0		1-0			2-0	1-0				2-0	1-0	1-2	4-0			1-3	1-1		3-1
Hartlepool	3-0			2-2	1-0		1-1			2-1	1-1		1-1	2-4	1-1	0-0	1-2	2-1	3-1	1-0		1-1
Lincoln	3-0	5-0	2-1	0-4			2-0	3-0	0-0	1-1					2-0	1-2	3-1	1-1	3-2		1-0	
Nelson	4-1	4-0	2-0	2-2	1-0		3-0	7-1	1-0	2-1		1-0			1-0	4-1	4-1		2-1		1-0	
New Brighton	4-0		3-0	0-0	2-1	2-1			3-2	4-0	3-2	3-1	4-1	5-0		5-0	3-1	1-1	1-0		3-0	2-1
Rochdale	0-1		2-1	2-2		5-0	2-1	3-1					3-1				4-1		2-1	3-0	3-2	3-1
Rotherham C	1-1	1-4		1-1	1-1		3-0	1-2	3-0	0-0	1-2	1-1	2-1	1-3					2-0		3-4	
Southport		3-0	5-0	3-0	0-2	2-0			1-1	3-1	3-1		4-0	1-0	0-0	2-0			1-0	1-0	1-0	1-0
Tranmere		5-2	4-1		5-1	2-2	0-1	1-2	1-1					4-3	0-0	2-0	1-3	1-0		0-1		2-0
Walsall	1-1	1-0	1-0	6-2		0-0	4-0	2-2	2-0	1-1			1-2	2-1	0-2	0-1	0-0	2-0			3-1	
Wigan		2-0			3-4	1-1	3-4	1-1	2-2	0-0	3-1	2-0	0-0	4-0	1-1	2-3		2-0	0-0			5-0
Wrexham	1-0		1-3	0-0	2-1	0-2	2-1	3-1	1-2	0-0	3-1	0-1	1-1	0-0	1-0		2-3				1-1	

Read the Chart horizontally to obtain the results of home games and perpendicularly for the
away games. The home team's score is given first in each instance.

THE LEAGUE Division I

	P	W	L	D	F	A	P
Huddersfield Town	31	16	5	10	54	22	42
West Bromwich Albion	30	19	7	4	48	26	42
Bolton Wanderers	31	16	7	8	57	29	46
Liverpool	30	15	8	7	51	41	37
Sunderland	32	16	12	4	49	41	36
Bury	30	12	6	12	41	39	36
Birmingham	31	13	11	7	33	36	33
Manchester City	32	11	12	9	61	56	31
Tottenham Hotspur	30	10	10	10	40	33	30
Notts County	29	10	9	10	26	21	30
Cardiff City	31	11	12	8	43	40	30
Newcastle United	33	12	6	15	48	30	29
Sheffield United	31	9	11	11	38	44	29
West Ham United	29	11	12	6	43	44	28
Burnley	31	10	13	8	41	54	28
Blackburn Rovers	30	9	12	9	38	45	27
Aston Villa	29	8	10	11	42	52	27
Arsenal	29	10	15	4	32	39	24
Leeds United	30	7	13	10	33	40	24
Everton	31	8	15	8	31	47	24
Notts Forest	30	5	17	8	21	54	17
Preston North End	30	7	21	2	25	61	16

THE LEAGUE—Division II

	P	W	L	D	F	A	P
Derby County	30	19	5	6	63	26	42
Manchester United	30	17	6	7	45	20	41
Leicester City	29	17	6	6	72	27	40
Chelsea	31	13	6	12	43	28	38
Portsmouth	30	13	7	13	39	40	33
Clapton Orient	31	12	11	8	33	29	32
Port Vale	29	13	11	5	34	37	31
Wolverhampton Wanderers	30	13	12	5	37	42	31
Hull City	29	11	11	7	43	37	29
Southampton	29	9	9	11	27	29	29
The Wednesday	32	12	15	5	39	47	29
Bradford City	29	12	12	10	30	37	29
Stockport County	31	10	13	8	29	40	28
Oldham Athletic	31	10	13	8	27	41	28
Blackpool	28	10	11	7	49	38	27
South Shields	30	9	11	11	33	33	27
Crystal Palace	29	11	13	5	33	38	27
Middlesbrough	30	8	11	11	27	35	27
Fulham	30	9	12	9	31	42	27
Stoke	31	8	16	7	23	35	23
Barnsley	29	7	16	7	32	15	21
Coventry City	30	7	17	6	34	68	20

DIVISION III—(Northern)

	P	W	L	D	F	A	P
Darlington	30	19	4	7	63	21	42
Bradford	31	14	7	10	68	33	38
Nelson	27	17	8	4	50	30	38
New Brighton	29	16	8	5	58	33	37
Southport	29	15	7	7	42	24	37
Rochdale	29	15	9	5	56	41	36
Lincoln City	30	13	10	7	39	30	33
Ashington	32	12	13	6	56	63	32
Doncaster	31	12	13	6	42	49	30
Crewe Alex.	30	10	10	10	39	52	30
Halifax Town	29	10	11	8	36	37	28
Barrow	31	11	12	6	39	48	28
Accrington Stanley	30	10	13	7	47	55	27
Chesterfield	30	10	12	8	35	31	28
Wigan Borough	31	10	14	8	42	48	26
Walsall	31	9	14	8	32	41	26
Durham City	29	8	11	10	33	50	26
Grimsby Town	30	9	14	7	34	43	25
Hartlepools United	29	9	12	8	34	45	25
TRANMERE ROVERS	28	9	15	4	40	46	22
Wrexham	31	7	17	7	26	49	21
Rotherham County	29	5	18	6	30	62	16

CHESHIRE COUNTY LEAGUE

	P	W	L	D	F	A	P
Port Vale	31	17	6	8	77	38	42
Hurst	31	17	7	7	80	43	41
Macclesfield	33	17	10	6	63	54	40
Ashton National	29	18	7	4	67	32	40
Stalybridge Celtic	28	16	7	3	62	31	38
Northwich	27	15	7	5	60	36	35
TRANMERE ROVERS	30	15	13	2	79	73	32
Crewe Alex.	29	14	12	3	62	49	31
Chester	30	12	13	5	40	60	29
Congleton	28	11	11	6	61	94	28
Whitchurch	31	10	14	7	44	67	27
Altrincham	30	11	15	4	38	74	26
Manchester N.E.	30	11	16	4	72	78	26
Winsford United	24	11	10	3	51	51	25
Runcorn	30	10	16	4	46	72	24
Mossley	28	10	14	4	45	57	24
Sandbach R.	28	10	13	5	47	55	23
Ellesmere Port C.	27	9	14	4	40	47	22
Middlewich	28	9	15	4	42	56	22
Witton Albion	28	8	14	6	37	55	20
Nantwich	25	7	11	7	51	54	21
Ellesmere Port Town	27	6	17	4	38	60	16

To-Day's Game : FACTS ABOUT OUR VISITORS.

This afternoon our Senior eleven entertain Rochdale, and as the Lancashire side, who have a glut of home matches during the remaining weeks of the season, are still in the running for promotion, we are assured of another "needle" tussle. There was a similar state of affairs obtaining last campaign, and as a result of the victory which our brought off against Rochdale, late on, we had a big say in the solving of the promotion question. As will be seen from the League table, Rochdale have a much superior record to us, but as we have faith in the "Blues" to rise once again to the occasion and bag a much needed two points.

Appended are the details of the Rochdale team:—

MOODY, H. (G); ht. 5-ft 10-ins; wt. 11-st. A native of Rochdale, he has been with club three seasons. Formerly played for Grimsby.

MASON, F. (R.B.); ht. 5-ft 10-ins; wt. 11-st. 8-lbs. Native of Birmingham, this is his first season with club.

BROWN, W. (L.B.); ht. 5-ft 11-ins; wt. 12-st. Born at Dundee, he was signed two seasons ago from a Scottish League team.

WILLIS, R. (R.H.); ht. 5-ft 10-ins; wt. 11-st 7-lbs. Born in Northumberland, he was signed from Dundee two seasons ago.

PARKES, D. (C.H.); ht. 5-ft 11-ins; wt. 12-st 4-lbs. A native of Staffordshire, and in fourth season. Previously with The Wednesday.

CHRISTIE, A. (L.H.); ht. 5-ft 9-ins; wt. 11-st 6-lbs. A native of Glasgow, and in first season with club.

CAMPBELL, J.(O.R.); ht. 5-ft 7-ins; wt. 10-st. He is a native of Blackburn, and is making a capable deputy to Tompkinson.

ANSTISS, H. A. (I.R.); ht. 5-ft 9½-ins; wt. 11-st. 7-lbs. Born in London, he was leader of the attack for some time.

OXLEY, W. (C.F.); ht. 5-ft 10-ins; wt. 12-st. Also hails from Northumberland.

ROSEBOOM, E. (I.L.); ht. 5-ft 8-ins; wt. 11-st. 7-lbs. Another Scot, he was born at Glasgow, and is in first season with club.

HUGHES, R. (O.L.); ht. 5-ft 8-ins; wt. 10-st 8-lbs. Another first season product, he is a native of Pelow.

ENGLISH LEAGUE—DIVISION III—Northern.

Tranmere Rovers v. Rochdale

AT PRENTON PARK

KICK-OFF 3-15 P.M.

TRANMERE ROVERS

1
BRIGGS

2
STUART

JACKSON
4

6
MALSTEAD

8
CHECKLAND

SAYER
5

7
CARTMAN

8
BROWN

9
DEAN

10
LITTLEHALES

11
RIMMER

Ref: Mr. F. SLATER (of Blackburn)

HUGHES
12

ROSEBOOM
13

OXLEY
14

ANSTISS
15

CAMPBELL
16

CHRISTIE
17

PARKES
18

WILLIS
19

BROWN
20

MASON
21

MOODY
[22

ROCHDALE

Any changes will be notified on Alteration Board.

67

TO-DAY'S SCOREBOARD.
F.A. CUP—4th Round—English League—DIVISION I.

	The Fixtures						1923-24 Results	1924-25 ½-Time
A	BLACKBURN R.	v	BLACKPOOL	...	...	...		
B	SOUTHAMPTON	v	LIVERPOOL	...	...	...		
C	SHEFFIELD U.	v	WEST BROM. A.	...	...	...		
D	CARDIFF CITY	v	LEICESTER CITY	...	...	...		
E	THE ARSENAL	v	BOLTON WAND.	...	...	..	0-0	
F	ASTON VILLA	v	TOTTENHAM H.	...	...	...	0-0	
G	BURY	v	EVERTON	...	...	...	—	
H	NOTTS FOREST	v	SUNDERLAND	...	...	...	0-2	
J	MANCHESTER C	v	NOTTS COUNTY	...	...	...	1-0	
K	NEWCASTLE U.	v	PRESTON N E.	...	...	...	1-2	
L	WEST HAM U.	v	LEEDS UNITED	...	...	...	—	

DIVISION II.

	The Fixtures						1923-24 Results	1924-25 ½ Time
A	BARNSLEY	v	STOKE	...	...	...	0-0	
B	BRADFORD CITY	v	THE WEDNESDAY	...	...	...	4-1	
C	DERBY COUNTY	v	CRYSTAL PALACE	...	...	...	5-0	
D	HULL CITY	v	CHELSEA	...	...	...	—	
E	MIDDLESBROUGH	v	COVENTRY C.	...	...	...	—	
F	PORTSMOUTH	v	STOCKPORT C.	...	...	...	—	
G	PORT VALE	v	OLDHAM ATH.	...	...	...	3-0	
H	SOUTH SHIELDS	v	CLAPTON ORIENT	...	...	...	1-1	
J	FULHAM	v	MANCHESTER U.	...	...	...	3-0	

68

Making great strides—

HIGSON'S
GENUINE ALES
Purest and Best.

THE HEAVIEST REVERSE.

On Wednesday last our Senior eleven visited Bradford, and as events turned out, suffered the heaviest reverse sustained thus far, the Park Avenue side running out victors by the wide margin of five goals to one. Without hesitation we say that the " Tykes " were the better side, and fully deserved the honours. In addition, it is our opinion that they have the finest forward line in the Northern Section, the vanguard being composed of Alf Quantrill, the ex-Preston North End player and English International, Myerscough at inside-right, and McDonald at centre, both of whom formerly played for Manchester United, McLean, a brother of the famous Scot, " Davie," and Peel at outside-left, for whose signature several clubs have been angling, but have kept off owing to the transfer fee asked being considered too high. In the opening half Bradford registered three goals, and the score did not flatter them. The opening quarter of the second period saw the trend of the game undergoing a complete transformation, for our boys revealed capital footwork, and had the home defence sorely taxed. Littlehales scored for us, and on two occasions Dean had wretched luck in not finding the net. Had the two chances referred to been goals, we would have been on level terms, and so well were our team playing at the time, that it is not unreasonable to say that probably we would have obtained others. As it was, Bradford came again, and before the close put on two further goals to make our discomfiture complete.

On March 28th, our Reserve eleven entertain Ellesmere Port Town here in a Cheshire County League game.

Touch-Line Topics : Interesting Faets and Figures - -

Darlington, who have signed on Hobson, the former Sunderland veteran, came back to their best form last week, and Wigan Borough knew all about it.

.. .. ..

The "Quakers" however, will have to give repeat performances if they are to hold their lead, as Nelson won at Halifax.

.. .. ..

Lincoln City, who did not pick up a single point during January, have had a merry February viz :— victories at Darlington, Barrow and Grimsby, and a draw against us here, while the remaining game at home, against New Brighton, was also won.

... ...

As the chewing-gum — cum — horn-rimmed spectacled fraternity would observe—"Some Going."

... ...

By notching four goals at Halifax, Nelson have wrested from us the honour of the hightest scoring visitors to the Shay ground this season.

... ...

Crewe, at Bradford, suffered their heaviest

reverse of the season, in being beaten by six goals to one.

... ...

Rochdale, who visit us this afternoon, have picked up thirteen points from seventeen away games this campaign.

ROVERS' MARKSMEN.

Appended is the detailed list of scorers :—

DIVISION III. (Northern)

Dean (23)	Littlehales (7)	Brown (2)
Sayer (2)	Fogg (2)	Campbell (1)
Stuart (1)	Moreton (1)	

CHESHIRE COUNTY LEAGUE

Jackson, J.R. (20)	Dean (9)	Fogg (9)
Rothwell (8)	Smith (7)	Birtles (7)
Millington (3)	Checkland (3)	Brown (2)
Littleshales (2)	Evans (2)	Sayer (1)
Jeffs (1)	Rutter (1)	Beswick (1)
Griffiths (1)	Newby (1)	Lewis (1)

OTHER GAMES.

1st Team—Rothwell (2), Sayer (2) Dean (1), Cartman (1), Littlehales (1) Campbell (1) Jackson (1)

2nd Team—Jackson (3) Evans (1) Birtles (1) Rothwell (1) Rimmer (1) Fogg (1)

Current Humour: *Smiles from Sundry Sources*

An old Negro was burning dead grass when a stranger approached and said : "You're foolish to do that ; it will make the meadow as black as you are."

"Don't you worry 'bout that, sah," replied the Negro. "Dat grass will grow out an' be as green as you is."

... ...

Mother : " I wish you would give up smoking, Bobbie."

Bobbie : " But it doesn't hurt me."

" You are too young to play with matches."

... ...

A Minister, calling one morning at the office of a solicitor with whom he was acquainted, was greeted thus : "Good morning, minister ; you see," pointing to two men seated in the office, " I have already two of your flock here, I hope they are not black sheep."

To this the minister replied : " It's not for me to speak of their colour ; but I'm thinking that if they remain here long they are likely to be fleeced."

To-day's Games.

League—Division 3—Northern

TRANMERE R.	(2) v	ROCHDALE	(1)
ASHINGTON	(4) v	HALIFAX T.	(0)
BARROW	(3) v	GRIMSBY T.	(1)
CREWE ALEX.	(1) v	WREXHAM	(1)
DONCASTER R.	(0) v	CHESTERFIELD	(2)
DURHAM CITY	(3) v	ROTHERHAM C.	(2)
LINCOLN CITY	(1) v	HARTLEPOOL U.	(1)
NELSON	v	NEW BRIGHTON	
SOUTHPORT C.	(1) v	ACCRINGTON S.	(0)
WALSALL	(2) v	DARLINGTON	(1)
WIGAN BORO'	(0) v	BRADFORD	(1)

The figures in parenthesis indicate the score in the corresponding game last season

Cheshire County League.

Mossley v Tranmere Rovers
Hurst v Ellesmere Port C
Sandbach v Ashton N.
Macclesfield v Port Vale
Chester v Congleton

SATURDAY, MARCH 14, 1925.

CHEHIRE COUNTY LEAGUE

Rovers v Chester

At Prenton Park   Kick-off 3-15 p.m

VENABLES BROS.

FOR

Quality, Design and Finish, in

FURNITURE & FLOOR COVERINGS

138, 140, 142
144, 146, 148 **OXTON ROAD**

Established 54 Years

Telephone 448

LEAGUE—DIVISION III.—Northern

Tranmere Rovers v. Hartlepools United

AT PRENTON PARK **KICK-OFF 3-0 P.M.**

TRANMERE ROVERS

1
MITCHELL

2 JACKSON 3 STUART

4 CHECKLAND 5 HALSTEAD 6 CAMPBELL

7 MORETON 8 SAYER 9 DEAN 10 BROWN 11 CARTMAN

Ref : Mr. I. JOSEPHS, Durham

HARDY 12 RICHARDSON 13 SMITH 14 COOK 15 BUTLER 16

NICHOLSON 17 STORER 18 FOSTER 19

OSMOND 20 ALLEN 21

COWELL
22

HARTLEPOOLS UNITED

Any changes will be notified on Alteration Board.

Established Half a Century

PHONE. 403

WILLIAM PYKE & SONS, LTD.

Watch-makers to the Admiralty

JEWELLERS. SILVERSMITHS, &c.

42-44 Market Street and 237 Grange Road

Withdrawal of the McKenna duties means a reduction in the price of Watches and Clocks

See the Windows

Waltham Watches from 72/6

After the Match go to

The CO-OPERATIVE CAFE

174 GRANGE ROAD,

(In the Centre of the Town)

Finest in Birkenhead

Teamsheet from the programme which marked Dixie's first Football League hat-trick on 25 October, 1924.
(George Higham)

Xmas Day's Game—FRIENDLY

Tranmere Rovers v Bolton W. Reserves

AT PRENTON PARK   **KICK-OFF 2-30 P.M.**

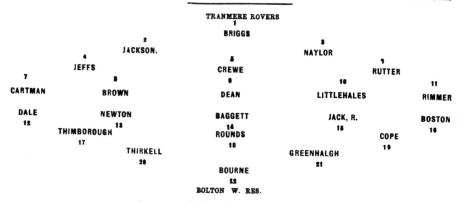

Any changes will be notified on Alteration Board.

Two for the price of one (tuppence!)—programme teamsheets from the
Christmas 1924 fixtures. Although shown in the Christmas Day line-up against
Bolton Wanderers Reserves, Dixie did not play.

(George Higham)

74

Saturday's Game—LEAGUE III.—NORTHERN

Tranmere Rovers v. Crewe Alexandra

AT PRENTON PARK

KICK-OFF 2-30 P.M.

TRANMERE ROVERS

1
BRIGGS

2
JACKSON

3
STUART

5
HALSTEAD

JEFFS

6
RUTTER

7
MORETON

8
SAYER

9
DEAN

10
LITTLEHALES

11
CARTMAN

Ref : Mr. J. R. MACFARLANE

12
HASSALL

13
TOMS

14
SULLIVAN

15
OLDACRE

16
STAFFORD

17
TURNER

18
NEVIN

19
MOSS

20
GOODWIN

21
WOOTON

22
SCOTT

CREWE ALEX.

Any changes will be notified on Alteration Board.

75

ENGLISH LEAGUE—DIVISION III—Northern.

Tranmere Rovers v. Barrow

AT PRENTON PARK   KICK-OFF 3 P.M.

TRANMERE ROVERS

1
BRIGGS

2   3
JACKSON   STUART

4   6   5
CHECKLAND   HALSTEAD   RUTTER

7   8   9   10   11
CARTMAN   FOGG   DEAN   LITTLEHALES   RIMMER

Ref : Mr. A. WIGNALL

ALFORD   VOWLES   DICKIE   LAYCOCK   WAINWRIGHT
12   13   14   15   16

LOWSON   BRELSFORD, T.   PAYNE
17   18   19

BRELSFORD, B.   BROADHURST
20   21

WHARTON
22

BARROW

Any changes will be notified on Alteration Board.

St. Valentine's Day Massacre! Programme teamsheet v Barrow
on 14 February, 1925,—another hat-trick for Dixie in Rovers' 4-1 win.

(George Higham)

DEAN FOR EVERTON.

Record Fee of £2,900.

(By "Forward.")

The biggest local sensation was provided on Monday when "Dixie" Dean, the Rovers' centre-forward, was transferred to Everton, and although many clubs were angling after this promising eighteen-year-old youngster, the "Toffies" have succeeded in sidestepping their co-bidders. The transaction was finally completed at the Woodside Hotel about half past six on Monday evening, and although neither the Everton nor Tranmere Rovers officials or directors are willing to disclose the amount of the transfer fee, I am informed, from a very reliable authority, that the exact figure was £2,900, and that the papers have been left with Mr. John McKenna, the chairman of the Football League, to allocate the proportion to the player. By the way, when the Rovers obtained nearly £1,000 from Stoke for Fred Groves, the latter received £60 as his share. Dean, however, has only had a little more than one season with the Rovers.

Opinions will naturally vary as to the wisdom or otherwise of the Rovers' directors parting with such a promising player, and one reason put forward is that hundreds of local enthusiasts will have patronised the games at Prenton Park with the main object of seeing Dean score goals, and will now transfer their allegiance to Goodison Park, and if they do the Rovers' club will suffer financially.

Although the fee may be regarded as a record for a Third Division player, I am personally of the opinion that the Rovers' directors should have held out for a sufficiently net amount to enable them to wipe off the whole of the £3,500 outstanding on the ground purchase scheme. Business is business, and whilst to some this may appear to be an exaggerated line to take, the fact remains that the Rovers' gates are bound to suffer, and the amount of the transfer fee should have been substantial enough to safeguard this contingency which, unless I am greatly mistaken, is bound to arise. In fairness to the Rovers' directors it should be stated that from financial reasons, especially when taking into account the debt on the ground, they have done what they thought best in the sole interests of the club, whilst again it must also be allowed that Dean himself was worthy of serious consideration, as Monday last was the final day allowed for transfers. during the present season.

Already several of the "grousers" have ventilated their opinions to me, and one individual who has not been seen on the Rovers' ground this season, as he is now an ardent follower of the Park, has declared quite innocently that the Rovers are not worthy of support, but seeing that he had arrived at this conclusion nearly twelve months ago, his protests can be ignored.

That Dean, owing to his goalscoring proclivities, was a draw at Prenton Park cannot for a moment be denied, but he was bound to be transferred sooner or later, and although I was given to understand from one of the club directors that he would remain a Rovers player at any rate for this season, I am not surprised at the sudden turn of events. I am, however, disappointed that the transfer fee was not greater than £2,900, as the chance of making a coup should not have been missed.

Dean is young, and being built on the right lines he should do well with his new club, who are badly in need of a centre who can score goals. Amongst the clubs who have been after him are Manchester United, Birmingham, Aston Villa, West Bromwich Albion, and Huddersfield, but local enthusiasts will be glad to know that he has been transferred to one of the Merseyside clubs.

Naturally many of the Rovers' supporters will be disappointed at his departure, but I hope it will be only a nine days wonder and that, like true sportsmen, they will wish Dean the best of luck.

(Birkenhead Advertiser, Wednesday, 18 March, 1925)

BIRKENHEAD NEWS, 30 JANUARY, 1924

ROVING ROVERS.

MEMORABLE JOURNEY BY ROAD.

Troubles in Abundance.

Chara Left In Ditch.

Like the cheap romances that form a feature of penny novels, the party of 16 players and officials of Tranmere Rovers might inscribe, after the record of their "strike-ing" experiences in the journey by road to fulfil their Third League engagement at West Hartlepool last Saturday, the popular proverb, "All's well that ends well." Certainly the details, which are facts and authoritatively vouched for, read more like fiction (writes "R.E.T.").

Owing to the railway strike it was found impossible to make the long journey from Merseyside to the far north-east by train, and so it was that at 9.15 on Friday morning the Rovers team with a reserve, and trainer Gaskill, in charge of Director R. Ledsom and secretary-manager Bert Cooke, boarded a covered in charabanc at the Liverpool Pier Head to cover the journey by road. It was expected that West Hartlepool would be reached before dark, and certain it is that none of the merry and contented party anticipated any of the events that were in store for them.

It was a beautiful morning, the bright rays of the sun tempering the nip in the air, and when Liverpool had been safely cleared, the party found joy in the wintry nature of the countryside. Everything passed off well during the first stretch of the journey, with the result that Skipton in Yorkshire was reached by 1 p.m. The route then lay across the bleak Yorkshire moors to Ripon, and the happy party were just at the height of their joy and praise of the scenery when the first of a series of events happened.

The chara had only got about three miles from Ripon when, in the narrow lane along which it was travelling, progress was blocked owing to a breakdown of a Ford motor van which proved to be the vehicle of a fruiterer and greengrocer, and was heavily laden with produce. There was nothing left to do but push the vehicle up the hill, and this task was entered into light-heartedly by the players, who however took reward for their labours by "winning" bananas, oranges and the like, what time the driver was engaged steering at the wheel. His song to the customers at the next village would inevitably be "Yes, 'I' have no bananas." The slight widening of the road allowed the charabanc sufficient room in which to pass, and the party all got aboard to make what was hoped would be more rapid headway. These were hopes that were soon to be shattered, for after travelling a comparatively short distance the engine began to "cough," and the warning bark of the exhaust foreshadowed trouble. The vehicle came to a standstill on a steep incline in the heart of the moors, and there was a delay of about an hour before the fault was remedied sufficiently to allow the journey to be continued.

By this time darkness was coming on, and as the vehicle was not fitted with headlights, the rate of progress was of necessity very slow as no light for steering purposes was given by the glimmer of the two oil lamps. The party resolved themselves into an emergency "Travelling Committee" to meet and deal with the situation and Frank Mitchell was unanimously appointed chairman.

A brief consultation resulted in the speedy decision that Jackson—popularly known as "Neddy"—should be entrusted with the onerous duties of acting as pilot and, if necessary, should the chara commence to run backwards to act as "scotch". To use "Neddy's" own words as to his chief duties they were "To walk in front with an oil lamp, swarm the signposts and otherwise ensure that the chara with its dignified load kept to the straight and narrow path."

It was about this time that someone mentioned that the Everton team had left for Harrogate by charabanc in charge of secretary T. McIntosh, and this was followed by the remark of Frank Mitchell that the Rovers were fortunate to have three "directors" with them. All knew that Mr. Ledsom as a fact was the only director present, and when asked to explain himself Mitchell said "Mr. Ledsom and the two 'Dunners' in front"—referring of course to the vehicle's oil lamps.

Ripon was eventually reached at 6.30 p.m., and there tea was partaken of during the halt of about half-an-hour. The journey to Stockton, the next important town on the road, was traversed at a snail's pace, and it was not reached until after 9 p.m. There the younger inhabitants made enquiries as to the identity of the Rovers, and were informed that they were the "Spurs". The nippers were most anxious to obtain the autograph of "Fanny Walden", and Jack Brown was introduced as the Tottenham idol. There was immediately a crowd round him, but all that was necessary was one autograph. And the reason—just that he penned as his signature "Nellie Wallace". It was not until 11.15 p.m. that the destination was reached, and despite the trying journey it was a happy party that partook of a hearty meal before retiring to bed at the Grand Hotel in West Hartlepool.

Saturday morning was spent in sight-seeing, and after the match the evening was also passed quietly and all retired to bed early.

On Sunday morning all were early astir, breakfast being served at 7 a.m., and the party embarked on the return journey at 8 a.m. The chara rattled along steadily for fully two hours when about four miles before reaching Ripon the engine again stopped. During the enforced delay of two hours Everton F.C. sailed past in their conveyance and many were the envious eyes that watched them pass out of view. The party eventually had to walk to Ripon, and the chara had to be towed by another vehicle into the town. In Ripon the Rovers came across the Rochdale team, who were making the return chara journey from Ashington. It was not until 3.30 p.m. that the engine of the Rovers' vehicle was put right, and when all had taken their places it was noticed that Mitchell was carrying a paper bag. Asked what it contained, he said "It's all right; it's just a bit of linseed. If the chara breaks down again I'll make a poultice and put it on the front to draw it."

Skipton, it might be mentioned was about forty miles distant, and it had been previously arranged that at the hotel there dinner should be ready for one o' clock. Skipton, however, was not reached until 6.30 p.m. It was a very black night, and the narrow roads with their dangerous and sharp turnings necessitated very careful driving. Things went well for a time, when suddenly and without warning the chara ran into a ditch on the left hand side of the road, and it was fortunate that on the inside there was a bank which prevented the vehicle from overturning.

No one was injured, and all took this episode as the crowning one of an adventurous week-end. Despite the efforts of the whole party, and aided by a few passers-by, it was found impossible to extricate the chara. It was ultimately decided to leave the driver in charge of the derelict vehicle, and the party walked to the nearest village of Gisburn—a tramp of four miles.

The village was reached at 10.30 p.m., and after waking up the village constable the party were directed to a telephone and got in touch with a Burnley motor firm, who promised to send out a relief chara for the stranded club. The occupant of the house with the telephone very kindly placed the drawing room at the disposal of the Rovers, and an impromptu concert was enjoyed.

The chara from Burnley arrived shortly after 1 a.m. on Monday, and fitted with powerful headlights it was able to travel speedily over the quiet roads, and the last part of the journey of over 50 miles was covered in splendid time, Liverpool Pier Head being reached at 3.45 a.m.

Secretary Cooke assures me that he has never had a more amusing time, and all the team took the many adventures in good part. Just another instance of the joys of the footballer.

∽≍∾

Although Dixie was not one of the party, I justify the inclusion of this sometimes hair-raising Hoffnungian saga as it happened during his short time on the staff of Tranmere Rovers and he must have heard all about it.

As well as being an inspiration to Dixie to join a club with a decent charabanc at the first opportunity (Everton were on their way home from a 1-1 draw at Middlesbrough), it is an enlightening and amusing cameo about the joys of travelling by road in the 1920s when 50 night-time miles in two and three quarter hours was regarded as speedy progress. Small wonder railways were the preferred method of getting to away fixtures.

It may seem strange that the main event, Rovers' predictable 1-2 defeat on the Saturday, is dismissed in two lines but there was the usual full match report elsewhere. (G.A.U.)

TRANMERE ROVERS v. BARROW.

THE PEOPLE WHO VISITED PRENTON PARK ON SATURDAY EXPECTED TO SEE A FOOTBALL MATCH - BUT AFTER SAYING GOODBYE TO THEIR NIMBLE BOBS

THEY MERELY HEARD TWO TEAMS ENGAGED IN A SHOUTING CONTEST

OFFSIDE !!

OFFSIDE!

THEY SHOUTED LOUDER

OF COURSE THERE WAS A LITTLE FOOTBALL, BETWEEN SHOUTS - FOR INSTANCE -

THE BARROW CENTRE KEPT TRYING TO KNOCK HOLES THROUGH HALSTEAD

UNTIL HE WAS "WARNED OFF"

ELLIS RIMMER.

OFFSIDE!

ROVERS WON, BUT THE HONOURS GO TO BARROW.

THEN WE HAD ON VIEW THE FINEST PAIR OF LEGS SEEN AT PRENTON THIS SEASON

THEY BELONGED TO RUTTER

FOGG OPENED THE SCORING

AND DEAN, PLOUGHING THROUGH THE MUD, DID THE "HAT TRICK"

GLOVER

Birkenhead News cartoon by Glover, 18 February, 1925, v Barrow.
Even in silhouette, there is no mistaking Dixie.

82

THE DIXIE DEAN INTERVIEWS

This is an edited transcript taken from Parts 1 and 2 of the interviews (six in all) with Dixie Dean conducted by BBC Radio Merseyside's Bob Azurdia. Introduced by a banjo rendition of "I wish I was in Dixie", they were first transmitted on 7 and 14 January, 1978.

My thanks to Bob Azurdia for his kind permission to include here these important and revealing insights as related by the man himself, unmistakably a native of Birkenhead. What these printed words cannot fully convey are Dixie's nostalgic and laconically humorous delivery, his natural modesty and his perfect Birkonian accent, quite distinctive from Liverpool's Scouse. Bear in mind too that this is direct conversational speech.

Dixie was 70 years old at the time and recalling events which were then already more than half a century ago. Quite understandably, his recollections were not always perfect—their value transcends the detail as they tell us something about his earliest days and then transport us back to those heady sixteen months at Prenton Park when Dixie, a mere youth of seventeen, was Tranmere Rovers.

～✕～

DD - I was born in 313 Laird Street, the North End of Birkenhead, and I went to the Laird Street Council School. From about seven or eight I was doing nothing only continually playing football. When I went to the Laird Street Council School I was playing for them from about 10 years until I left school, 14 years of age. But I was never a great schoolboy. As a matter of fact, I didn't have any knowledge much of anything at all in those days, except football. My own school, Laird Street School, I played for four years for them and two seasons for Birkenhead Schoolboys. Outside right in the first season for the Schoolboys and centre forward in the second season. Then, of course, there was school leaving but I'm afraid I got no further in the school than giving the chalks out and giving the ink out. I am one of those, I suppose, that I was a dunce if it came to that. Even in those days when the papers used to come out on a Saturday there was only just the one result that I used to look for and that was Everton. I never looked for Liverpool. Just Everton.

BA - *What about brothers or sisters?*

DD - I had no brothers, no. I had six sisters and I was the next to the youngest. That was where—talking about the heading and such like, there was an old chapel at the back of our house and I used to get a ball and throw

83

it up onto the roof. I had a goal already put out on the wall of the chapel. I used to throw this ball up, wait for it to come down then head it against the wall in the position where the goalkeeper wasn't, sort of thing. That to me was a great thing. I used to enjoy every moment of that and then again passing the ball.

You wouldn't have to worry about having somebody else to kick it back for you. You'd be running up alongside the wall from about ten or twelve yards away, running the length of the wall and back again. I've done that quite a few times, kicking this ball against the wall, receiving it, chesting it down or thighing it down and thumping it back against the wall, which was very good practice. Just down below in Brassey Street School in Birkenhead was coming along then the boy Rimmer, Ellis Rimmer—who also was capped with me at one time for England—he was their star turn.

BA - *What about any coaching influence in any way?*

DD - No, I had no-one at all. As a matter of fact I can say that what I learned I taught myself. I could spend many an afternoon just with that chapel roof and the wall. Or, if I could get fixed up in a match anywhere, where they used to just pick two teams, put their coats down for goal posts and so on, and get as much football as I possibly could.

I was selected to play for the Birkenhead Schoolboys Trial Teams and when you'd finished a trial team I'd borrowed a bicycle so as I could get back down to Birkenhead Park to play for my school team. Then in the afternoon was a team called Melville I used to play with. I scored six in the first trial match, six in the schoolboys—Laird Street School— and then six with Melville in the afternoon; so it was a good day's work. I got eighteen in the three matches in one day.

BA - *Of course, you were talking all the time now about days just about the end of the First World War, I would say, because you would be about eleven when the war ended and life obviously was very different in Birkenhead. How different was it?*

DD - I was pretty lucky in that respect because my mother had two fish and chip shops and lucky in a sense that I built up a pair of good shoulders. I used to turn the spuds for her for both the shops and the quicker you got them done, of course, the sooner you could get out and play football. Now then if you didn't do them properly you'd have to sit there for probably another hour or so and eye the potatoes. So it was just as well to give them a good drumming. Talking about enjoying yourself in those days, I was pretty lucky there again because we used to get passes for picture houses when we put the bill up in the chip and fish shop window—and the sisters of mine used to encourage me a bit with dancing. I used to go to dancing classes and I turned out quite a decent bit of a dancer as well and especially a bit of tap dancing. I used to put that in for the lads later on in life at Everton or wherever we were. Oh, I loved tap dancing. I mean, even now when I, well since before I had the last operation, I used to still have a go. There was many a time, especially when we were away special training, that I used to start performing for them. Ah, yes.

BA - *Was your dad away during the war? Was he in the forces perhaps?*

DD - No, he was on the railway. Reserved job. Yes.

BA - *Can you remember the war at all or would you be too small? Can you remember, for example, whether any Zeppelins were coming over or anything?*

DD - Oh I remember the war quite well because the people next door to the fish and chip shop, they had a milk round. We used to be up at 4 o'clock then in the morning and go up to a place outside of Birkenhead, Burgess's Farm, and get the milk from them and then bring it down and deliver it round Birkenhead. You were allowed an hour off school in those days for this milk round. We also had an allotment. We had to grow our own potatoes and vegetables and all that sort of thing. Oh, I remember it very well, yes.

I remember that War in particular because from where I lived and the main North West Army Camp was only a mile and a quarter away, and that was at Bidston. That was where all the drafts used to come right down Laird Street, right down to the ferry and then they'd either board their ships or go across to Liverpool—and that was them on their way to France.

I think we enjoyed life a lot more than they do now, even if it was only on an old street lamp post—make yourself a swing and go swinging round there. Somebody looking round to make sure the copper wasn't coming. Not only that but we used to have toss schools (that's what they used to call "pitch and toss") and always have two or three good keepers looking out. I think we enjoyed ourselves a lot more then.

BA - *You also had to get up early in the morning to cross the river to go and get fish, too?*

DD - Yes. I used to go across to St John's Market in those days and buy the fresh fish for the mother's shops. The people then knew that they always had the fresh fish there. Well, that would save them sending anybody older on account of the fares. The fares on the trams in those days (there was no buses) was a ha'penny and then across on the train. You could

85

have a day's work in really, but you never thought anything of it because I was quite a big boy. I've had to go down to the tram depot two or three times with my mother because, under 14 years of age, I could travel for a ha'penny—after that it went to adult fare. I went in and my mother played hell with them and had the letter from my headmaster at Laird Street School to prove that I was still under fourteen.

Once I knew about these fellas getting paid for playing football—which I thought was great, being equipped with everything, boots, trousers, jerseys and what else have you—I'd have played for the love of the game, in their boots, of course.

The day I left school was on the Friday; mother took me down Grange Road in Birkenhead, the shopping place, and bought me a nice new pair of overalls. They were the first long trousers I ever had on. Then on the Monday I started serving my time on the Wirral Railway as an apprentice fitter—my old chap had made all the arrangements. I was interested in it because right against from where I was working, and you did have to work in those days, was the Wirral Railway football ground; all I had to do was to climb two fences and get in a kick somewhere now and again even if it was only for a Thursday team on a Thursday afternoon. If they turned up one short, I could always wriggle into there. The reason why I could do this was the two other apprentice fitters with me didn't like the night job. They worked the 2 'til 10 and 6 'til 2; I done the 10 'til 6 so that I could play football during the day; and, of course, during the night you could always have an hour's sleep, you could always have a doss and that just suited me down to the ground.

BA - *And how long did this go on then, how long were you apprenticed on the railway?*

DD - Well I'd served just on two years and my old general manager was a man named Martlew. Now Mr Martlew's two sons were both doctors and directors of New Brighton Football Club—they'd asked me several times would I like to go and have a trial with them. But I just had one ambition then and that was to get to Everton. Any rate I went to play with Pensby; that was just out in the country from me at the time. If you missed the bus, you had to run out there. I used to get a nice little bit of tea and two shilling. Of course, the two shilling was supposed to pay for the bus—but we used to use Shanks' pony.

BA - *And what sort of money would you be on as an apprentice incidentally?*

DD - I was on 12 shilling for the night job. Yes, I used to save that in my lemonade bottle. What I could of it.

BA - *And give some to your mum, no doubt?*

DD - Oh yes. Aye—she'd be satisfied with about 7s.6d and I'd have the other.

BA - *What about your first pair of football boots though Bill, how old were you when you got your first pair of real boots?*

DD - Well that was the mother again. She took me out and had me fitted for them. I'd be about nine or ten or something like that. Then, of course, as I grew, they knew then that that was going to be a career.

BA - *And they were keen on you playing football, your parents, and interested as well?*

DD - Yes. Oh yes. Both of them. Yes.

BA - *Did you ever manage to go and see Everton or Tranmere Rovers?*

DD - Not once. No, nor Tranmere. Then, I had a match on every Saturday afternoon. I wouldn't miss a match; I mean if I went there and found they had a full team I'd would probably run up and down the line flagging, anything at all as long as it was football. When I went out to Pensby, I was just getting stripped after the match and a chap comes in to me and he said "How would you like to have a trial with Tranmere?" I thought, "Well, this is a bit of a stepping stone." So I told him—I said, "Yes, I wouldn't mind." He said, "And if you do come off they'll sign you professional." It was a chap named "Dump" Lee who used to be the main scout of Tranmere.

I went and they played me the very next week—in a Cheshire County League match at Middlewich in Cheshire. I scored a couple of goals and, from then on, it seemed to me to be a bit easier than playing, with Pensby because with Tranmere reserve team you had better players, which it stands to sense, Cheshire League players; and with Pensby, of course, I was doing more donkey than I should do. From the Cheshire League side I got into the Third Division side.

I went during the close season and signed with them but I didn't get any summer wages. Then I signed for £4.5s.0d. When the season opened I was put into the first team. I scored a goal in the first match. I think we won it 2-1, I'm not quite sure. I went on with the first team about a third of the season and then I got an injury which put me in hospital for a while. I had to have an operation. When I came back, I kicked off then with the Cheshire League side to have a run out and we played at Middlewich, scored a couple of goals there, and came straight back into the first team.

BA - *In all you played about a season and a half for Tranmere before, in March 1925, you actually moved to Everton?*

DD - March 1925, yes. I landed home this day—I'd been out to the pictures and my mother was there. She said would I go down to Woodside Hotel and meet Mr McIntosh, the Everton secretary. So I did. I went down to the Woodside Hotel and there was Mr Tom McIntosh, the Everton secretary. He shook hands, he told me what it was all about. He said, "We would like you to come to Everton." I said, "Well that's it." I hardly believed it. That was the greatest delight of my life because that was all I'd been waiting for. I signed on the Wednesday and Mr McIntosh turned round and said to me, "You will be playing against Arsenal on Saturday at Highbury." "Oh blimey," I thought, "that's a bit of a jump." But any rate that was it. I went over, met the players the next morning on the Thursday, introduced to them all. I felt right at home, right away. Yes.

BA - *You say you started on wages of £4.5s.0d. What about bonuses, incentives, expenses or anything to supplement your income.*

DD - No, you got £1.0s.0d if you won and 10 shilling if you drew—then with the Cheshire League side you were on 10 shilling and 5 shilling, which, of course, in those days was pretty decent. But when I come to look through and learn a little, I believed that Tranmere should have been paying me, when I was playing with the first team, £6.0s.0d. I made one or two enquiries but I didn't go any further with it and stayed on £4.5s.0d.

BA - *Did you immediately give up your apprenticeship on the railway?*

DD - Oh yes, I had to finish on the railway because I'd signed full-time you see. It was full-time training. You'd be there on a Sunday morning, if you had any injuries, and then you'd be there on Monday. Now, your week's training begins on a Tuesday morning, and you'd probably do about 10 miles—it might be 12 miles—from the Tranmere Ground straight up the Borough Road, across over the Thornton Road and back through the Prenton Playing Fields and that was your morning roadwork.

Then, in the afternoon, you would lap once or twice and then I would definitely go onto sprints which I wanted—30 yard sprints all the time so as you'd be quick off the mark. You were there again on Wednesday morning, you were there Thursday and Thursday afternoon and then you would go in and do a few sprints on a Friday morning. Then you'd rest up until the Saturday match.

BA - *Who was in charge of the team at this time?*

DD - A chap named Gaskill. We used to call him Old Bill Gaskill. And then, Jimmy Moreton who used to play outside right with Tranmere. He also went on the training staff.

There was a secretary there, Bert Cooke. This man took everything on his own shoulders. He took the lot, as regards signing players on, paying players, diddling players. He took it all on his own shoulders. I know that because he diddled me. He promised my mother and dad that I'd receive £300 out of the £3,000 that Everton had paid for me; he said he'd kick me off with a bank book and I'd have 300 quid in it. When I received a telegram, I went along to the ground, about a fortnight later, he handed me a cheque for £30. So I turned round to him and I said, "You've made a mistake here. You've left an 0 off." He said, "I'm sorry Dean but that's all the League would allow you." I knew very well that he'd made these conditions with my people.

So I went across and seen Mr John McKenna who was Chairman and President of Liverpool FC. I told him what had happened and his only words to me were, "Dean," he said, "You've signed that haven't you?" I said, "Yes sir." He said, "Well I can't do anything for you now." He said, "I could have done but I'm afraid not now—you've already signed." So that was that and I'm afraid I didn't really feel terribly sad about leaving Tranmere because I did always want to get away and just get to the one and only club—Everton. I mean that's been my club since I was a kid. I'd have played for nothing there.

BA - *What about this injury you had, because it was the sort of injury which could have marred you psychologically for life because, at the age you were at, about seventeen I think at the time, well it was pretty devastating. What happened and how did it all happen?*

DD - Well, we were playing Rochdale, in a League match, and Rochdale had this centre half, a chap named Davy Parkes, one of these big six foot two fellas and a big strong man. I went down the middle a couple of times and got two early goals.

BA - *This was at Prenton Park was it?*

DD - That was at Prenton Park, yes. And Davy Parkes, as I passed him going down the field, he said " Tha'll get no more bloody goals today, you've finished." So right away I said to him, "By the looks of you, you've finished, you've had it." I'm afraid that he was a great tipster because when I did come sailing down the third time, he kicked me where I didn't want kicking and I'm afraid that if the ground had of opened that day I only wish it would have swallowed me. But any rate, I had to go into the hospital and have a testicle out. So they strap you down there to this here flat bed affair and you've got to wait until this thing stops swelling. Then they gave you a little touch of the old gas lark and away you go. But while this thing was swelling, I turned round to the specialist and told him. I said, "You'd better hurry up—if this thing blows up it'll blow this bloody hospital up." At any rate, it didn't affect me in any way afterwards, in after life.

BA - *And how long did it take before you were actually playing again?*

DD - Oh only about five week. Yes. Well you see I was a stone lighter then. I could sprint a bit then. As a matter of fact, I've never wished anybody any harm but I always said to myself that I'd come across that man somewhere or somehow and I'd get a bit of revenge for it. And I did. I met him in Chester about seventeen years later. He sent me a pint across the bar. When I asked the barman who sent it he pointed to him and I couldn't quite place the face for a time. But I did. And then I done his face up and they took him to the hospital, so we're evens! That's about the only time that I've ever, it was the only time as a matter of fact, and ever since, that I ever retaliated. The only thing I used to do was turn round to the man .. I had fifteen operations, by the way, throughout the footballing career.. the one that broke a bone or gave me a broken rib or a broken shoulder blade or whatever it was—I used to just turn round and say to them while I was laying there, "Has this done you any good?" and that was it.

BA - *What did you do in your spare time apart from playing or practising?*

DD - I was always one of those lads into keep fit. I used to play a lot of golf. I learned my golfing tricks at the Wirral Ladies' Golf Club. I used to go caddying there and you were swinging clubs all day long. And, of course, once I got into the football game, the first thing I done was buy myself a set of golf clubs. I got down to scratch and won quite a few competitions. I really loved golf, yes. I used to go dancing a lot. I learned the ballroom dancing but I'd never had any special partners or anything like that. I wasn't what you'd say over keen on girls.

BA - *Not more than any other lad of seventeen or eighteen?*

DD - No. Just might meet one at a dance and have two or three dances with her—well they used to think they were courting you or something. I had a good time while I was with Tranmere because I used to go to all these here different functions on the Town Hall—Police Ball and the Farmers' Ball. Quite a lot of them.

BA - *And what about the cinema? You mentioned going to the cinema before. Can you remember any particular types of films you liked in those days because that would have been just before the talkies?*

DD - Yes, well they would be cowboy pictures or something like that. No love stories and all that caper—no it used to be the Westerns. Well, of course, they had quite a number of characters at Prenton. We had Jackie Brown who was then the present international for Ireland. The other side of him playing inside to me was Stan Sayer and then the centre half was Fred Halstead. Those lads could go on the ale a little bit and they certainly used to. We had teachers in the team.

We had a chap named Frank Checkland, who was a teacher across in Liverpool. Also a chap named Jackson. During this time, we also had Pongo Waring taking chocolate and cigarettes round the ground. Pongo used to tell the supporters that he was as good as me and he'd prove it to them one day. Which he did. It was about five years later but in any case he'd done what he said he would do. During all this time there was also Ellis Rimmer; he played for the Schoolboys with me and then came and signed with Tranmere while I was there. I didn't play a great deal with Ellis because my transfer was coming off, you see. But later on in life—Ellis, of course, went to Sheffield Wednesday,—we played together for England. We played against Spain at Highbury. They certainly had a tough side at Tranmere and we had Kenny Campbell, goalkeeper, but we had a tidy side.

BA - *Anyone particularly who took you to one side when you where at Prenton and gave you any advice?*

DD - No. Oh no. No—they'd rather stay in the Halfway House those fellas. They didn't bother about that. No I can say really that I taught myself. Sammy Chedgzoy, when I went to Everton, would lay on one or two things for me and show them actually done, which I picked up. I think he is about the only one. At Tranmere you had nothing like that there. They had no time then for such things as that.

BA - *When did you first hear that there were people looking out for you from senior clubs? Did you find the scouts coming and chatting you up and so on?*

DD - No. Well the first time was when we went to play Ashington; they were in the Third Division in those days. We stayed in Newcastle overnight. On the Saturday morning Bert Cooke took me to St James's Park and we were met there by the Newcastle directors, chairman, or whatever, and they showed me all round the ground. In the meantime, they were telling me how I would fit in there and how I wouldn't fit in and so on. That never impressed me at all. I just said yes and no and thank

DD - you very much and hope I'll see you again some time. Which I did later on. Then this Cooke asked me would I care to be transferred to Newcastle and I said, "No thank you very much." "Well," he said, "there's not only Newcastle, but there's the Villa, Bolton and the Arsenal. You can go to any of those clubs." I said, "If you don't mind I don't wish to go to any of them. I'm quite alright where I am at present." I didn't fancy Newcastle. That one and only team was Everton, of course.

BA - *So you bided your time until finally, in March 1925, you got this call to go down to the Woodside and you agreed to sign almost at once presumably?*

DD - I did sign right away. As a matter of fact, I didn't even ask how much are you going to give me or anything like that. I had no idea 'til I got paid on Friday and that was on the Wednesday. Then on the Friday I packed a little case and off I went to London, to Highbury.

BA - *So, within the first couple of days you played in your first First Division game?*

DD - Yes. On the Saturday. I scored a good goal as I thought and so did the goalkeeper because this ball came over and I headed it in. It went into the top corner of the net and the goalkeeper just caught it then, as it fell, and threw it up the field to be kicked off. But the referee was pointing that the ball hadn't gone over the line or something or other—so I didn't get the goal.

BA - *Who else was playing in the Everton side that day, can you recall?*

DD - Yes. Old Sammy Chedgzoy outside right; Hunter Hart, he got a cap, he was a Scotch cap. A chap named Kennedy we bought from Manchester United; Alec Troup, we bought from Forfar, outside left—a great little player that. He could put that ball within an inch of my head. Billy Brown, another Scotchman. Jock MacDonald another Scotchman, David Raitt another Scotchman and the goalkeeper was Tommy Fern.

BA - *You went over to Goodison Park for the first time then on the Friday, did you? And were you welcomed by the team and club and the captain and so forth?*

DD - Yes. I went over on the Thursday morning to do some training. Well in those days Everton had one or two hard knocks and two were centre forwards, by the way; one fella named Jack Cock—Everton bought him from Chelsea; and a fella named Jimmy Broad from Stoke. They looked over at me. One of them said to the other, "It looks as though we will be away from here pretty soon now." As a matter of fact, they were—it was only about two or three weeks later they both went and I took over from them.

BA - *Did you team up with any of the lads fairly soon at all or were you particularly friendly with any of the Everton team?*

DD - Not right away—excepting for old Sam Chedgzoy. As I say, Sammy gave me a little bit of tutoring and he seemed to take a great fancy to me.

BA - *Well what about your first home game at Goodison Park—can you remember that one?*

DD - Yes. That was against Aston Villa. I scored in that match as well.

BA - *You had said before that you had no great sense of occasion when you first joined Tranmere. You more or less took it for granted that this was part of the logical process towards joining Everton. Did you have any great excitement once you had this blue jersey on or any great anticipation for your first First·Division games? Was this in any way different from joining Tranmere?*

DD - No. I just knew that I'd come off at Everton.—it had been there since I was a child and I just seemed to know that I could do something and, of course, it didn't take me long to prove it there. Because after I had played three or four times with the first team, they put me back with the Central League team.

BA - *So you were actually dropped once and you only played one reserve team game then?*

DD - One, against Bradford City. I think we beat them about nine and I got seven of them. The following week they put me straight back in and from then on I never looked back.

BA - *Again, coming back to the build-up for the start of this new career in the First Division.*

DD - On the Saturday morning my mother, before she brought me a cup of tea, would always bring me in a spoonful of Phosferine and this happened every Saturday that she was alive when I was at it. Then I'd have an egg or something like that. I wouldn't have to go over to the match, then, so I'd wait and have a bit of boiled fish round about 12 o'clock and a bit of toast. Then when I was going from my home down Park Road North to Duke Street Park Station, it was there where the crowds were starting to go across and in those days with the old trams there was queues and queues of them waiting, either in Water Street or down at the Ferry or wherever the special buses ran from. And then, going up with them, in these old jam jars, as they used to call them, I'd be with all the supporters—especially the gang off the railway, my old man's crowd; they must have had about 25 or 26 tickets a week, buckshee.

BA - *There was quite an atmosphere crossing over there?*

DD - Yes, nothing, you know... it was all good patter and all that sort of thing.

BA - *Ever get caught in the crowd at all, did you ever get held up and thought that you were going to be late?*

DD - Oh once or twice when there was a real good match on. I was always told by the Everton Board if anything did arise, anything like that, I was to jump in a taxi but I had no money for taxis then really but that's what they always told me. Jump a taxi.

BA - *In those days too then you were on £6.0s.0d a week?*

DD - Yes plus £2.0s.0d bonus.

BA - *£2.0s.0d for the First Division?*

DD - £1.0s.0d with Tranmere but £2.0s.0d and £1.0s.0d a draw with Everton.

〜✖〜

The popular theory on how Bill Dean got his nickname is that Tranmere Rovers fans gave it to him because his crinkly hair and swarthy appearance put them in mind of the American coloured people from down south in Dixie.

Now there is evidence that 'Dixie' could in fact have been a "sounds like" for 'Digsy'.

Certainly this is the name attached to Dean in a book called *Up Our Lobby*, published recently by Wirral Libraries and written by Bill Houldin, a Birkenhend contemporary of the great centre-forward.

We are indebted to Mr G. A. Upton, of Southport, for bringing this to our notice. Intrigued by the new information, he wrote to Mr Houldin and received the following reply:

"The name 'Digsy' was just one that we grew up with and so never questioned. However, your query prompted me to do a little bit of research . . . and referred to the *Birkenhead News* report of Bill Dean's funeral.

"The reporter quotes a lady contemporary of Bill's. When questioned about the name, she said: 'When Bill Dean was doing the chasing in a game of tag, he would catch a young lady and he would dig is fist into the girl's back, and for his pains acquired the name 'Digsy'.

"The few old neighbours of ours and Dean's I have spoken to have dismissed out of hand any suggestion that 'Dixie' had connotations of colour. I, too, say this is bunk."

Everton's programme v Arsenal on 7 May, 1988, celebrated the Diamond Anniversary of Dixie's 60 League goals in 1928. It included the author's letter about the more likely origin of the soubriquet "Dixie".

PROGRAMME 1d.

Tranmere Rovers Football Club

(Founded in the reign of Queen Victoria)

Telephone—**Birkenhead 1821**

●

Ground—**PRENTON PARK.** Office—**14 PRENTON RD. WEST**

Chairman/Hon. Secretary-Treasurer,
R. S. TRUEMAN

Trainer Coach
W. RIDDING

Christmas Day (Dec. 25)

FOOTBALL LEAGUE (NORTHERN DIVISION)

TRANMERE ROVERS v. LIVERPOOL

Kick-off 3-15.

A HAPPY CHRISTMAS AND A PROSPEROUS NEW YEAR TO ALL OUR PATRONS AND PLAYERS, AND MAY NEXT YEAR SEE US ON THE WAY TO AN EVERLASTING PEACE.

To-day we welcome as visitors old friends in Liverpool, and we give a special welcome to Chairman R. Lawton Martindale, Messrs. W. McConnell, Walter Cartwright, Ronnie Williams and Manager George Kay.

Founded in 1892, twelve years later than ourselves, Liverpool have a grand record, and although the F.A. Cup has so far eluded them, their league record is something of which they have every reason to be proud.

Since their formation they have been F.A. Cup Finalists 1913-14 ; Champions of Football League (Division I) 1900-1, 1905-6, 1921-2, 1922-3 ; Champions of Football League (Division 2) 1893-4, 1895-6 and 1904-5. The record for the Anfield ground, 61,036, was against ourselves in the F.A. Cup on January 27th, 1934.

This term Mr. Kay has moulded a particularly successful team together, and but for a couple of unexpected slip-ups would have finished champions. In order to secure second place they must beat our youngsters this afternoon.

A good game is anticipated, and may the better team win !

R. S. TRUEMAN.

Tranmere Rovers v Liverpool, Christmas Day, 1942—Wartime match programme.
Dixie is down to guest for Rovers but did not make it.
(Peter Bishop)

96

Tranmere Rovers
(Blue)

R. YEARDSLEY

RADCLIFFE (2)   OWEN (3)

GLIDDEN (4)   L. HUGHES (5) (Capt.)   HODGSON (6)

L. L. ASHCROFT (7) LAMB (8)   DEAN W.R. (9) ROSENTHAL (10) O'NIELL (11)

C

HULLIGAN (11) HAYCOCK (10) DONE (9) FAGAN (8) (Capt.) DORSETT (7)

PELLING (6)   KEEN (5)   KAYE (4)

GUTTERIDGE (3)   WILLIAMS (2)

HOBSON

Liverpool
(Red)

Referee—**J. E. Thomason,** Chester.   *Linesmen*—**E. Lawrence** (Wirral)
J. H. Clayton (Liverpool)

SUBJECT TO ALTERATION

SPECIAL NOTICE.—Every endeavour is made to field sides as advertised but owing to the calls of H.M. Forces and National Service, changes are unavoidable.

BOXING DAY
To-morrow at Prenton Park.   Kick-off 3-15.   FOOTBALL LEAGUE CUP

TRANMERE ROVERS v. EVERTON

SATURDAY, 2nd January, 1943, at Prenton Park.   Kick-off 3-15.
Rovers "A" v. Rootes
(with Dick Platt)

BIBLIOGRAPHY

Football League Handbook (1924-25)

Tranmere Rovers programmes 1924-1925—collection of George Higham

Ellis Rimmer's "Agreement for hire of a Player" when he signed for Tranmere Rovers on 12 September, 1925 (courtesy of Warwick Rimmer)

The Encyclopaedia of Association Football—Maurice Golesworthy (1963)

Dixie Dean : The life story of a goalscoring legend—Nick Walsh (1977)

The Dixie Dean interviews with BBC Radio Merseyside's Bob Azurdia (1978)

Everton : A Complete Record 1878-1985—Ian Ross & Gordon Smailes (1985)

The Survivors : The Story of Rochdale A F C—Steven Phillipps (1990)

A-Z of Tranmere Rovers—Peter Bishop & Gilbert Upton (1990)

New Brighton : A complete record in the Football League—Garth Dykes (1990)

The Fabulous Dixie—Phil Thompson (1990)

Tranmere Rovers : 1881-1921—Gilbert Upton (1991)

Local Studies Libraries:-

* Wirral
* Calderdale (Halifax)
* Chesterfield
* Cleveland
* Durham (Darlington)
* Nelson
* Northumberland (Morpeth)
* Rochdale
* Sefton (Southport)
* Shropshire (Whitchurch)
* Trafford (Altrincham)

TRANMERE ROVERS
1881-1921
by Gilbert Upton

I n 1991, after six years' painstaking research, Tranmere Rovers' statistician and historian, Gilbert Upton, himself produced this in-depth account of the first forty years of the premier Wirral club from the days when it was founded by the Tranmere Wesleyan Chapel as Belmont through to its debut in the Football League in 1921-22 season. As well as a record of Rovers' progress, it sets the story in its wider soccer and local history contexts.

A book of 180 pages, including many and varied illustrations, it re-writes and re-discovers the history of the club's early days, pin-points when it was actually founded (not 100 years before the club celebrated its centenary in 1982) and provides unrivalled details of Rovers' emergence from the pack of local clubs in Wirral through its progressive ideals and dedicated management. Contents include:

* the arrival of soccer on Merseyside
* the original Tranmere Rovers whose name Belmont assumed
* the men who started the club, and their backgrounds, including *"The Father of Tranmere Rovers"*
* their local rivals and how they were vanquished, including the renegade Birkenhead F C
* chronology listing every game (1369 in all) from foundation until joining the Football League
* a statistical summary of these years by leagues, cups etc
* traces the growth in attendances and gate receipts
* all first XI league tables from 1889-90 until 1920-21
* F A Cup appearances and goalscorers pre-1921

W hether you are an ardent Tranmere fan or someone interested in the rise of association football, to order this unique and intriguing book, please send a cheque for £7.50 per copy (£9.50 sterling overseas) including postage and packing, to:

G A Upton, 8 Cumberland Road, Southport, Merseyside, PR8 6NY.

"..a labour of love..one of the most detailed accounts of the origins and development of a professional club.. as much a work of local history as a book about football..carefully produced, easy to read and very modestly priced.."

(The Footballer).

"..a both readable and scholarly work.. much commentary on the society of the times and the role of football in the community .. for the statistician too there is plenty here.

It is unlikely that there will be a better early history of the Birkenhead club."

(Association of Football Statisticians).